Marketing Accounting Services

Marketing Accounting Services

Robert J. Listman

DOW JONES-IRWIN
Homewood, Illinois 60430

© DOW JONES-IRWIN, 1988

Acquisitions editor: Susan Glinert Stevens, Ph.D.
Production editor: Lynne Basler
Copyediting coordinator: Jean Roberts
Production manager: Bette Ittersagen
Compositor: Western Interface, Inc.
Typeface: 10/12 Melior
Printer: BookCrafters, Inc.

ISBN 0-87094-897-0

Library of Congress Catalog Card No. 87–71360

Printed in the United States of America

1 2 3 4 5 6 7 8 9 0 BV 5 4 3 2 1 0 9 8

This book is dedicated to two very special people whose lives have so favorably influenced the lives of others: My mother, Dolores Listman, and my wife, Judi, who value the needs of others beyond their own.

PREFACE

Nine years ago a colleague asked me to develop a marketing-oriented practice development seminar for the Indiana CPA Society. I am a marketing educator by profession, and the challenge of applying marketing theory and practice to the then burgeoning professional services field was appealing. That initial seminar led to the development of many others. Soon I found myself advising a cross section of public accounting firms and other professional service suppliers. I learned a lot from these clients and have attempted to incorporate their wisdom throughout this book. These encounters were also fascinating to me because I felt an intellectual closeness to these clients, for I am also a marketing consultant selling my own form of intangible service to the business market. Clearly, I could relate to my clients' questions and concerns, and as I progressed in experience, the idea of writing a book in marketing accounting services kept creeping into my consciousness with reckless regularity.

Being both a marketing educator and a consultant has greatly influenced what I perceived to be important topics to address in this book, for marketing is an analytical discipline that greatly relies on initially determining what to consider before deciding what to do. Therefore, I do not promise any cookbook solutions to problems or any tried and true formulas for success. They do not exist! What I have tried to give you is a way of approaching a problem, alternative strategies and techniques, and the most important of all, what to consider before deciding what to do. Marketing is a learned art whether it concerns an accounting practice, a manufactured good, or a retail venture. However, there are several unique considerations involved in the marketing of a professional service, and I have also addressed these throughout the book.

My sincere wish is that you find this book of value and that it positively affects the relationships between you and your clients. For our relationships with others are among the things in this world that matter the most. In the production of a service, how we relate to our clients and fulfill their needs is what effective marketing is all about.

Acknowledgments

Many individuals exerted both a direct and indirect influence upon the creation of this book. To the administration and faculty of Valparaiso University, I wish to extend my appreciation for the research leave that allowed me the time to write this book. To my colleagues in the College of Business Administration, thank you for your concern and support. In particular, I owe a special acknowledgment to Jim Ehrenberg, CPA, chairperson of the Accounting Department at Valparaiso University. Nine years ago Jim asked me to help conduct a practice development seminar for the Indiana CPA Society. This initial exposure led to a growing involvement in the field of marketing professional services. Thank you, Jim. I also extend a special thank you to Kim Green for her invaluable help in the preparation of this manuscript. I wish to express my appreciation to John Wyu, CGA, of J. W. Wyu and Associates, Ltd. for his thoughtful and valuable critique of the manuscript. His sage advice made this book eminently more readable. To my wife, Judi, and to William G. Bunting, a deep-felt appreciation for their faith in me and for all that they have taught me over the years.

Robert J. Listman

CONTENTS

Why Many Advertising Campaigns Are Ineffective. What Makes Advertising Successful. Developing an Effective Campaign: *Selecting the Right Media. Specific Media to Consider.* Selecting an Advertising Agency. Notes.

Marketing Accounting Services

PART ONE

Developing a Marketing Orientation: A Strategic Decision

"If we want to formulate plans that will be successful in tomorrow's world, we should study who has tended to be right more times than not in thinking about tomorrow, and who has tended to be wrong. If you do so you may find that it was often the marketer who most clearly foresaw future business opportunities, rather than the technicians, the scientists, and the general managers.

"When you reflect on this it makes good sense, because marketing people are constantly striving to find out what people want and then to look for ways to satisfy these needs. It is an immutable fact that tomorrow's winners in our business or any business will be those that understand clearly that our only reason to exist is to create a customer, and that customers are created by finding better ways to help individuals and corporations solve their problems."

Walter B. Wriston, *retired Citicorp chairman, quoted in the* American Banker, *September 28, 1984, p. 4. From an address given to a Peat Marwick seminar. Excerpted from James H. Donnelly, Jr., Leonard L. Berry, and Thomas W. Thompson,* Marketing Financial Services *(Homewood, Ill.: Dow Jones-Irwin, 1985), p. 20.*

Understanding the Role of Marketing

"It is not until an abstract concept, a new way
of thinking, is evaluated and operationalized
that it truly begins to live."

Accounting as both a discipline and a profession has been constantly changing since its beginnings. Technological developments, new and increasingly complicated governmental regulations, theoretical developments, and clients' needs for more readily accessible and precise financial information are some of the factors that have affected this evolutionary growth. In accounting, as in most professions, when growth is evolutionary, the process of change is subtle and continuous. However, change can also be of a revolutionary nature and far more difficult for organizations to deal with. At the least it is an unsettling experience, but more frequently when revolutionary change is immediate and dramatic, a type of organizational inertia can result. For a firm to prosper, this inertia has to be overcome, but this unplanned change has created a unique dilemma. Management must abandon the traditional while embracing the new and unproven. If the new and unproven is not welcome, or if managers are unaware of how to adjust to the change, a befuddling lack of activity often results. Yet, to return to the traditional is neither possible nor prudent. This is what has happened to the public accounting profession, and it has been unsettling to some firms while catastrophic to others.

THE CHANGING COMPETITIVE ENVIRONMENT

In 1977, the Supreme Court, in *Bates* v. *The State Bar of Arizona*, ruled that the ban against advertising legal services that had existed since 1908 was an unwarranted restriction of trade.[1] The process of revolutionary change had begun, and many long-standing promotional restrictions, like dominoes, would fall in a type of chronological order. Directly following the Supreme Court ruling, the Federal Trade Commission and Justice Department turned their watchful eyes toward trade restrictions set by other professional associations in such fields as medicine, dentistry, and public accounting. These associations were told to rescind their long-standing promotional restrictions or face the certain prospect of being actively prosecuted. These professional associations resisted the change at first, but their legal counsels wisely advised that in this legal battle they would surely be the losers. For the American Institute of Certified Public Accountants (AICPA) and state accounting societies and boards this ruling subsequently led to the rescinding of their long-standing bans against advertising, direct solicitation of competitive clients, and self-designation as experts.

This revolutionary change was accompanied by evolutionary changes in the market, such as an oversupply of public accounting firms, an expansion of the depth and breadth of technical service offerings, and more targeted, aggressive competition from the "Big Eight" firms. Furthermore, general accounting firms were more frequently forced to compete against more specialized accounting firms offering an array of technical services to specific client segments, such as doctors and dentists. Regional firms were also accelerating their practice of merging or buying out the smaller, local firms to quickly expand their business in a new community. Many firms found it difficult to compete against these larger firms, who offered both a wider array of services and a more prestigious image to clients. All these developments intensified the competitive climate of public accounting. Unfortunately, change came too quickly and many firms were unsure of how to market their practices in the changing environment. The more staid practice development lore was clearly not working as well. Most firms had little experience in this new form of aggressive, targeted marketing. However, the underlying question then and today is: What does one use as a viable substitute to the traditional lore? It is one thing to aspire to a new way of thinking and doing business, but quite another to effectively execute the change.

THE NEED TO MARKET
PROFESSIONAL SERVICES

These are tumultuous times for many public accounting firms, because the aforementioned developments are still evolving. The need to market public accounting services has never been more acute. For many organizations, whether they become a casualty statistic or a viable, competitive firm firmly rests in their ability to become marketing-oriented.

The irony of the situation is that public accounting firms have been discreetly marketing their practices for years. Public accounting firms have traditionally engaged in a narrow array of laid-back, professionally sanctioned promotional practices. An acceptable range of promotional activities was the tried-and-true practice development lore to follow. Firms did not advertise, but they did mail "informative" newsletters to a wide array of commercial and municipal organizations. They did not openly solicit clients from competitive firms, but it was professionally acceptable to become highly visible in community, social, and business organizations for the purpose of recruiting prospective clients. While it was against the AICPA Code of Ethics to designate oneself as an "expert" in any given field, it was common practice to identify an area of "expertise" to a prospective or existing client. Therefore, to now debate the ethics of marketing public accounting services is an academic exercise in rhetoric! Public accountants have traditionally thrown their organizational hats into many commercial rings.

There always was and always will be a need to market services, because service quality alone is not enough to ensure market success. The old adage, "build a better mousetrap and the world will beat a path to your door," is erroneous. Product or service quality is requisite for market success, but it does not ensure it! Firms must learn how to market their services in new ways, more consistent with the dynamic competitive environment of the 1980s. Therefore, the contemporary question that needs to be answered is not whether or not it is ethical to market public accounting services. Rather the question is: What does marketing entail, and how does one strategically market one's services?

CONCEPTUALIZING WHAT
MARKETING ENTAILS

Marketing means different things to different people. Some equate marketing with a type of slick Madison Avenue imagery, and they confuse advertising and the more pervasive sales promotional techniques with marketing. Others equate marketing with salesmanship, publicity, or public relation techniques. Yet all of these, while being marketing functions, are not synonymous with marketing. However, since these functions just happen to be the most visible evidence of promotional activity, some CPAs erroneously conclude they are all that marketing entails and hastily reject marketing as not applicable to their commercial endeavors.

Yet, the intrinsic nature of marketing is such that it is synonymous with professionalism. Why is this true? Because marketing's driving principle is one of client satisfaction. The implicit functions of a marketing-oriented public accounting firm are:

1. Assessing clients' needs and wants and developing services and delivery systems that fulfill them. This also includes the necessary follow-up work after an engagement to ensure client satisfaction and subsequent retention.
2. Ensuring that the method of producing the service is truly satisfying clients' needs. This means delivering the appropriate service, at the right time, place, form, and at a fee consistent with customer needs.
3. Developing accurate, informative, and persuasive communication between prospective and existing clients and the firm. This means employing different communication media that are best suited for particular communication tasks.

Some uses of different communication media firms are advertising (mass communication that is paid for), personal selling (interactive, personalized communication), publicity (mass communication that is not paid for), and sales promotions (short-term activities or events used to stimulate demand). Some examples of sales promotional devices used by public accountants are tax planning seminars open to the public or specific, highly topical, workshops for client employees or referral sources.

A WORKING DEFINITION OF MARKETING

Philip Kotler and Paul Bloom, two noted marketing scholars, offer this definition of marketing in their text, *Marketing Professional Services:*

> MARKETING is the analysis, planning, implementation, and control of carefully formulated programs designed to bring about voluntary exchanges of values with target markets for the purpose of achieving organizational objectives. It relies heavily on design-

ing the organization's offerings in terms of the target market's needs and desires, and on using effective pricing, communication, and distribution to inform, motivate, and service the markets.[2]

It is important to note the component parts of this definition in order to identify the implicit functions of marketing. First, **marketing** is essentially an analytical process relying on the traditional management functions of analysis, planning, and implementation. When developing a marketing strategy, one has to rely on facts, interpret situations, and project the marketplace's reaction to a proposed program. This is definitely more of a creative, but learned art, than a science. Science relies more on empirically tested laws and propositions that both predict and explain.

Second, marketing is not designed to be manipulative because it seeks to bring about voluntary exchange relationships between both parties. In order to become commercially successful, both clients and the offering firm must be satisfied with the outcomes of the engagements. Anything less than this is bound to be a commercial failure.

Third, marketing activities are aimed at satisfying the needs of one or more preselected groups of clients rather than at trying to satisfy the needs of the aggregate market, which can seldomly be done very well or very cost effectively.

Fourth, marketers must consider both the organizational objectives of the firm and the needs of the target markets when formulating strategies. This is reflected in the modern day **marketing concept** that can be summarized in this phrase: Satisfy the needs and the wants of your consumer while achieving a profit for the firm. This does not imply that a firm is an unwilling slave to its clients. Rather, there has to be a harmonious relationship between the needs of the firm and the needs of clients. Consequently, effective marketing often starts with an audit of what the firm has to offer, its capabilities, what it can deliver with a consistent level of quality, as well as an identification of the needs of target markets.

It is also important to realize that frequently clients may not be able to readily communicate their needs. Needs can be apparent, but it is the service supplier's responsibility to satisfy these implicit needs with the effective execution of a service. Consider the consumers of a generation ago who had a need for an easier, less labor-intensive method of washing clothes. Would these consumers have been able to communicate to a firm what a proposed new product, a washing machine, should look like? Needs have to be first determined, then analyzed, and the job of the marketer is to develop products or services that fulfill these needs.

Finally, this definition of marketing clearly includes product or service development, pricing, and distribution functions, as well as promotion. Marketing managers term service development, pricing, distribution, and communication functions as the **marketing mix.**

MARKETING MIX CONSIDERATIONS

Marketing is far more than merely promoting an existing service. Effective marketers must blend the four elements of the marketing mix together, so as to form a cohesive marketing program. To use a contemporary saying, marketing mix elements must "hang together" so that the sum of the individual parts is always greater than the whole in marketing (see Figure 1–1). Why is this true?

FIGURE 1–1

Marketing Mix Components

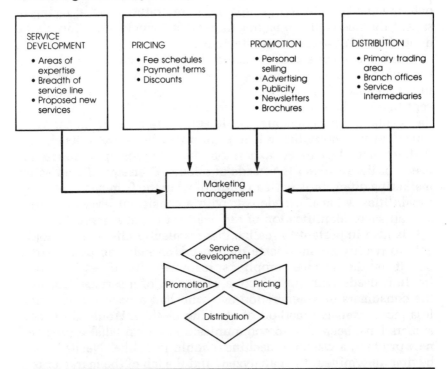

Because marketing people must initially develop, and then blend together, each component of the marketing mix. Frequently adjustments have to be made in separate elements, such as fee schedules or service offerings, in order for the entire program to fit the needs of the target market.

In fact, when marketing professionals refer to a **marketing strategy,** they are referring to a specific marketing mix targeted toward one or more market segments. Selecting and implementing an operational marketing strategy will be the sole topic of discussion in Chapter 5. However, the important point to remember is that marketing is far more than just promotional planning. Equating marketing with promotion greatly limits the contribution marketing could make to an organization.

MARKETING DUTIES OF PUBLIC ACCOUNTING FIRMS

Table 1–1 is a listing of some typical marketing duties that reflect analyzing a practice from a marketing mix perspective. This listing is taken from a 1975 survey of Virginia-based public accounting firms who reported performing certain marketing practices. These reported percentages are not projectable to the present, nor are the reported practices an all inclusive listing. Yet, they do describe some classic marketing duties all public accounting firms ought to be performing.[3]

The last category of duties, Marketing Research, in Table 1–1 deserves special attention. Specific diagnostic information needs to be periodically compiled from prospecting forms, quarterly billing sheets for major service areas, client evaluation reports, and from externally based marketing research studies. What to consider when developing such a system, as well as the type of information required, will be thoroughly discussed in Chapter 3. However, at this point it is important to realize that marketing decisions have to be based on factual information. Marketing information is necessary when developing and assessing the efficacy of a marketing strategy.

There are literally hundreds of examples of service firms and goods manufacturers who have unsuccessfully based their corporate strategies on what they thought the customer wanted. For example, Travelers Insurance Inc. believed that consumers placed a high value on the perceived degree of technical expertise of larger firms with a greater depth and breadth of service offerings. Only

TABLE 1-1

Marketing Practices of 73 Virginia CPA Firms

Activity	Percent of Firms Performing
Service offering	
Periodically reexamine services offered	81
Determine which new services to offer	80
Estimate size of client base for new services	49
Determine share of market for present services	43
Establish written goals and policies	43
Define specific client groups to be served (e.g., retailers, manufacturers, professionals)	29
Communication	
Develop an overall information approach, identify major users, and select methods for reaching them	17
Develop specific informational approaches (e.g., brochures, seminars)	27
Develop public relations programs understandable to nonaccountants	26
Location	
Analyze potential locations for new offices	40
Evaluate volume and trends at existing locations to see if a move is indicated	38
Fee structure	
Evaluate fee policies on a systematic basis	90
Collect information on competitors' fees on a systematic basis	17
Market research	
Evaluate clients' needs	90
Study why people "buy" their services	37
Study who key influences are in engaging the services offered	46
Train and motivate firm members to feed back information about clients' needs and problems	77
Determine the firm's "image" among clients and the general public	84
Study profit trends by service categories and client categories	59

Source: William R. George and Richard M. Murray, "Marketing Practices of CPA Firms," *CPA Journal* 45 (October 1975), pp. 33–36. Reprinted with permission of the *CPA Journal*, copyright 1975.

through a thorough and well-executed marketing research study did management learn that consumers most valued personalized service. There was also some evidence to support the stereotyped adage that large corporations do not offer personalized service. The moral of this story is that you can be in the business a long time and still misinterpret the underlying and evolving needs of your clients.

Consider for a moment this question: Why do clients engage the services of your firm over those of your closest competitors? Ask several members of your firm this question, and you may well be surprised at the diversity of opinions you obtain. Additionally, for certain types of services, what are some of the underlying purchasing motives? Do consumers most often engage public accountants for tax preparation work for mere convenience, because of their own lack of technical expertise, or because of a belief that they will receive a greater refund? Certainly, motives will vary, but frequently there are dominant motives that the majority of consumers within a market segment possess and act on. The firm has to determine and address these motives before obtaining an engagement.

UNIQUE DIFFERENCES IN MARKETING PUBLIC ACCOUNTING SERVICES

Marketing professional services is different from marketing goods.[4] Marketing theory does not necessarily change, but organizational settings, legal and ethical restrictions, and the needs of clients do. There are several fundamental differences per se in marketing goods versus services, as well as some unique considerations in marketing public accounting services. Collectively these differences mean that different strategies and approaches need to be taken. Let's examine the most important differences.

1. The Intangible Nature of Your Services. Services are consumed, not possessed. While goods are tangible entities, services are intangible. A good is an object, a device, a thing; whereas, a service is a deed, performance, or effort.[5] The performance of many services has to be supported by tangibles, just as many goods have intangible service components as part of their basic product offering. Unfortunately, many CPAs too frequently confuse their service with their production process. For clients, the service is an intangible entity, difficult to conceptualize and, therefore, more problematic to evaluate. Compounding this problem is the fact that accounting services, because they are so technical, are often less tangible than other services. This makes them more difficult for clients to relate to. Figure 1–2 ranks several services that vary in how intangible they are to consumers. Accounting services are at the far right of the continuum and therefore are less tangible than the others.

Remember, a service cannot be inventoried, tried on for size, tasted, or smelled, but it can and will be evaluated by clients. Public accounting firms must therefore carefully analyze the nature

FIGURE 1-2

How Tangible Services Are to Customers

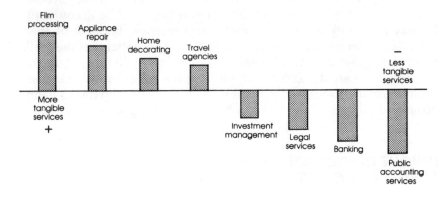

of what is being sold. The decision to purchase a service and retain a firm depends on whether the execution of a service matches consumer expectations. A requisite for market success is to identify the needs of clients, as well as their underlying motivations, and then compare actual experiences to clients' expectations. This means that the firm has to have some follow-up evaluations concerning clients' satisfaction with service encounters. For it is far too easy to confuse technical service attributes with buyer needs and to erroneously conclude that sophisticated technical support facilities, lower fees, or skilled staff, provide evidence that a firm is meeting buyers' needs and expectations.

2. Client Involvement in Distribution and Consumption. Unlike goods, services are generally sold and then simultaneously produced and consumed. Goods are produced, sold, stored, and later consumed. This difference is far more than semantics. The student taking courses, the guest at a hotel, and the client involved in setting up a new accounting system are all experiencing the service they are simultaneously consuming and producing. Because clients are often involved (although in varying degrees) in the production of the service, the "how" of service distribution is crucial. When marketing goods, great emphasis is placed on distribution decisions involving both the where and when of distribution—that is to say, the right place and right time. When marketing services, however, the right way or "how" is oftentimes the most crucial decision.[6]

Client retention is based on the buyers' satisfaction with both the production and the consumption of the service. The classic example is the firm that promises not to interfere with the client's normal office routine when conducting an audit. When the audit crew arrives, office flexibility is replaced with a rigid adherence to normal audit procedures by busy auditors who have time schedules to maintain. The observable results are a thorough disruption of the client's office routine. When this occurs, the partner in charge of the audit quickly learns just how important the production process is to the retention of a client. This is true despite the technical quality of the audit or the usefulness of the information to the client. The point here is the importance of assessing the delivery system through the eyes of your clients. In marketing a service, there has to be a lot of management by walking around and paying close attention to the nitty-gritty of the distribution system, rather than merely assessing the technical quality of the service.

3. The Problem of Maintaining Quality Control.   It is far easier to maintain quality control when producing goods versus services. Statistical process control systems, routinized production processes, and other such control procedures help ensure an acceptable, uniform level of quality when producing goods. When manufacturing goods, the reliance is on machinery, production processes, and routinized procedures. When producing services, the reliance is more on staff interacting with clients. Most consumers of goods, for example, are not very concerned about the intricacies of the production run, the appearance of the workers on the line, or technical processes to which they have difficulty relating. However, in marketing accounting services, clients' evaluations of the value of the service are specifically influenced by their perceptions of the delivery personnel. Therefore, it is quite understandable that clients equate their evaluations of the delivery system (staff and processes) with the value of the technical service, which they cannot very objectively or realistically assess.

It is therefore the responsibility of CPAs to help clients better identify their need for select services and the value of alternative service offerings, as well as to help them establish more objective evaluation criteria. This is a quality control function. Staff members have to be taught to assume this responsibility, because for many the trap of just performing the service and leaving is all too real. Maintaining quality control means more than just ensuring that technical work is flawless; it also means creating within your staff the expectation that assessing service quality from clients' perspectives is a part of the quality control process.

4. Duties of the Staff in Marketing the Practice.   A common error that many public accountants make is to assume that only management of the firm is responsible for marketing a practice. Some firms erroneously believe they can totally centralize the marketing function with a director of marketing or delegate it to all divisional partners. Additionally, within many firms a large number of delivery personnel feel that promotion, prospecting for new clients, qualifying service needs, closing the engagement, recruiting referral sources, and other such marketing functions are not really a part of their job.

I recall one consulting engagement with a large regional firm where the managing partner took the "marketing pill." He hired a director of marketing so the firm's staff personnel would not have to be bothered with marketing the practice and could better concentrate on the production of the service. The new change was a dismal failure, and the managing partner rationalized his actions by stating: "Most of us have had no training in marketing; we are not salespeople, and no interest in becoming ones. We are accountants, and what we have to sell is time. The name of the game is to log in chargeable hours and not waste staff time in activities we cannot charge out, or perform well." While this sounds reasonable, effective practice development just doesn't work that way. Rather, the professionals who are delivering the service have to be actively involved in the marketing of the service. After all, they are really the ones best suited to determine clients' needs and to assess the needs of the firm.

When marketing professional services, marketing is more of a line function, and as such it cannot be very effectively assigned to a staff expert who is not involved in the production of the service. Effective marketing means satisfying the needs of clients and helping them to identify potential and existing problems. When manufacturing goods, it is far easier to split functions into production versus marketing. However, this will never be the case in marketing a professional service. Staff have to learn how to market the services they produce. This may well mean expanding the firm's training program to include tips and guidelines on how to prospect; how to select, cultivate, and develop referral sources; how to close engagements; how to qualify client needs; and other such marketing activities.

Indeed, it is necessary to turn producers into sellers. There can be a director of marketing who has the responsibility to help put into operation marketing strategies, formulate marketing plans, coordinate activities, develop promotional support materials, and help train staff personnel in classic marketing functions. Yet, marketing will still remain the function of every member of the firm who comes in contact with clients. Some call this level of involvement "grass roots marketing" or "internal marketing." Whatever the term, producers of technical services have to be involved in the marketing of the service. There is no pragmatic, operational way to abdicate this responsibility to a functional staff specialist in marketing.

5. Ethical Considerations in Marketing a Practice.   The adage "old ways die hard" is true of the marketing practices of many local and regional firms. Even in today's competitive environment many firms would consider it a violation of personal ethics to directly solicit clients from a competitor. Others feel the same way about advertising and/or promoting their expertise in some facet of public accounting. Despite the rescinding of long-standing bans by state and national associations, many CPAs still believe that these practices are unprofessional. For some firms this places severe restrictions on their ability to market their practices. The problem becomes severe when these firms are placed at a competitive disadvantage to others. In essence they are deciding to return to a competitive environment that no longer exists. Compounding this problem is the inescapable conclusion that traditional practice development lore is not going to be as effective in a changing market.

A prerequisite for growth in a highly competitive market is to differentiate a firm from competitors. This is accomplished through adjustments in marketing mix elements, such as the breadth and quality of service offering, fee schedules, distribution (how the service is delivered), and promotion. Merely doing a better job for clients or offering a better value is not enough if what you have to sell is not marketed effectively. Consequently, it is important for CPAs to examine objectively the implicit pros and cons of previously banned promotional methods, rather than summarily to reject them as unethical or unprofessional.

6. Problems in Estimating and Servicing Demand.   Unlike goods, services cannot be inventoried for future consumption. This causes a particular problem during peak load months. If a client is in need of a specialized service, there is no warehouse to go to and no safety stock to draw on. Services are also labor intensive, and this means that staff personnel have to be hired, trained, and available to provide the service when demanded.

Demand, although difficult to forecast, has to be anticipated. Because it is frequently quite difficult to estimate market demand for certain types of services, many firms find it necessary to assume a type of reactive versus proactive posture. This can and does have a negative impact on growth and client satisfaction. Effective marketing has to be concerned with the smoothing out of demand as well as alternative ways of servicing demand. Some options that other professional service suppliers have been employing are cross training of personnel to perform a wider range of customarily demanded services; hiring paraprofessionals and part-time staff to help service seasonally high demand (such as during tax season), shifting demand to slower periods through promotional and price incentives, and preplanning and scheduling regular service offerings at a time when the firm is better able to service demand.[7] These are marketing considerations that should be addressed in a firm's marketing plan.

7. A Limited Base of Marketing Expertise. Today, public accounting firms have a limited base of experience in classical marketing functions, such as advertising. Such professional publications as the *Practical Accountant* and such associations as the AICPA offer both articles and seminars concerning various marketing activities. These are quite helpful, but the literature does not offer many case situations of what has worked for some firms, while failing for others. As is true in many industries, determining what to do and then how to do it is a result of managerial skill, luck, and a process of trial and error. What works well for one firm in one marketplace may fail in another.

NOTES

1. Terence A. Shimp and Robert F. Dyer, "How the Legal Profession Views Legal Service Advertising," *Journal of Marketing*, July 1978, pp. 74–81.

2. Philip Kotler and Paul N. Bloom, *Marketing Professional Services*, © 1984 (Englewood Cliffs, N.J.: Prentice-Hall, 1984), p. 4. Reprinted by permission.

3. William R. George and Richard M. Murray, "Marketing Practices of CPA Firms," *CPA Journal*, October 1975, pp. 33–36.

4. Aubrey Wilson, *The Marketing of Professional Services* (London: McGraw-Hill, 1972).

5. Leonard L. Berry, "Services Marketing Is Different," *Business Magazine*, May–June 1980, pp. 24–29.

6. G. L. Shostack, "Breaking Free from Product Marketing," *Journal of Marketing*, April 1977, pp. 73–80.

7. Leonard L. Berry, Valerie A. Zeithaml, and A. Parasuraman, "Responding to Demand Fluctuations: Key Challenges for Service Businesses," in *1984 AMA Educators Proceedings*, ed. Russell Belk et al. (Chicago, Ill.: American Marketing Association, Series #50), pp. 231–34.

Creating a Marketing-Oriented Public Accounting Firm

"The **marketing concept** in American
business has grown increasingly popular, but
it is still misunderstood. In essence its basic
principles are (1) find out what the client
wants and needs, (2) develop or improve
service offerings that fulfill those wants and
needs better than ever before, (3) find ways
to induce clients to choose your products
and to keep on choosing them, while
earning a profit for the firm."

Organizations tend to have a dominant orientation, such as a production, financial, or a marketing orientation. This orientation is a
natural outgrowth of the value system of the organization and is
very evident in what organizations consider when making decisions. A **production orientation** essentially means that an organization places the greatest emphasis on making and distributing
products or services, which are easy to produce as well as distribute. Management looks at customers as existing to buy the firm's
output rather than the firm existing to serve customers' needs.

Public accounting firms with this production orientation seldomly identify and evaluate the needs and wants of specific client segments in any formal manner. Marketing is not a driving force within the firm and is not an integral part of the decision-making process. In fact, service quality is usually assessed exclusively from internal review, rather than from matching client expectations with the actual performance of the service. The end result is that service development essentially becomes a production rather than a marketing responsibility.

A firm that has a **financial orientation** also fails to incorporate marketing into its decision-making process with any impact. What to produce and distribute is primarily based on predetermined and short-term financial outcomes. In such environments the better outcomes eventually evolve into mandated goals to obtain, rather than a predictive indication of how well some longer-range strategy is working. Individual and/or divisional performances are then measured by looking at cash flow projections and returns on invested time and capital, with a pronounced failure to consider the needs of customers. Unfortunately, this has happened all too frequently in American business over the last decade, and public accounting firms have not been immune to this common malady.

Firms that place too much emphasis on maintaining rigid financial standards (such as profit minimums and attaining some high percentage of total chargeable hours) often fail to identify opportunities for growth. The environment does not allow for risk taking, and the more talented entrepreneurs become disgruntled and leave. This can be devastating to any organization, but especially so for public accounting firms that sell advisement-related services. The important conclusion to remember is that in any exchange relationship both the needs of the clients and the needs of the firm must be satisfied. To do any less than this will eventually affect the growth of the firm.

THE ROLE OF MARKETING IN A PUBLIC ACCOUNTING FIRM

Now let's take a look at what a **marketing orientation** offers management. Marketing, as a business function, is not implicitly any better than accounting, finance, or production, but it is different. The paragraph at the beginning of this chapter describes the marketing concept. Firms that operate on this concept are said to be market-driven firms. The marketing concept implies that firms organize their activities to satisfy both the needs of the firm and the clients. Because of this unique client orientation, marketing orientation is more receptive to determining changes in the market, assessing clients' needs, and determining what competition is doing than the other orientations. CPA firms embracing this orientation are better able to assess clients' needs, and develop services that satisfy both the needs of the clients and the firm. To be a marketing-oriented firm does not mean that a firm fails to consider what production- and financial-oriented firms consider. Nor does it mean that a public accounting firm has to engage in highly visible mass communication campaigns as package goods companies do. Rather, a marketing orientation means the firm has implemented the marketing concept so that it becomes an organizational value for employees to achieve.

Table 2–1 illustrates some fundamental differences between a marketing orientation and a production orientation. A necessary first step in marketing your own practice is to assess the managerial orientation of your own firm using this simple but revealing contrast. Chances are that some of the functions your organization is performing are more of a marketing orientation than a production orientation. This is frequently the case, because rarely does any one firm in a changing market rigidly adhere to all tenets of a particular orientation. Therefore, it would be helpful to approach this listing in Table 2–1 in a kind of plus-minus fashion, so as to determine the general orientation of the firm. You may well find that you have a marketing orientation in only 4 out of the 10 listed functions (four pluses and six minuses). This more detailed comparison will help you determine what has to be changed in order for your firm to become a more marketing-oriented firm.

A fair question you may be asking yourself at this time is what will a marketing orientation do for your firm? For one thing, it will help you compete more effectively against specific competitors appealing to a similar client mix. Second, it will help you manage your practice, so growth will be planned rather than characterized by the peaks and valleys many firms experience. Last and most important, a marketing orientation will improve the quality of service you deliver to your clients.

Also, it should be pointed out that every exemplary company mentioned in the popular book, *In Search of Excellence*, is a marketing-oriented company, or market-driven firm. This is quite understandable because being a market-driven firm means satisfying the needs of customers, while achieving organizational objectives as well. These excellent companies did not get this way by chance, but rather by design. That is the challenge that may very well face your organization today.

TABLE 2-1

A Marketing versus a Production Orientation

Function	Marketing Orientation	Product Orientation
1. Attitudes toward clients	Clients' needs are pivotal in determining firms' policies.	Clients should be glad we exist because of our high quality service and cost consciousness. Firm sells what it can produce.
2. Service development	Firm produces what clients need and will purchase.	Firm sells what it can produce.
3. Profit orientation	Profit potential is a key consideration when developing services designed to satisfy clients' needs.	The residual that remains after costs have been covered.
4. Marketing research	Designed to assess clients' needs and determine how well the firm is meeting these needs.	Designed to determine clients' reaction, if used at all.
5. Role of advertising	Acquaints prospective clients with the benefits of a service or benefits of employing the firm.	If used at all, lists staid service features, office hours and location, and other production-based information.
6. Service innovation	Focus is on marketplace and determining new growth opportunities consistent with resources of firm.	Focus is upon technological developments.
7. Focus of top management	Assess needs of clients, determine growth areas, monitor client satisfaction, and provide marketing leadership.	Determine ways of selling what the firm wishes to produce. Assess service quality only from an internal review perspective.
8. Fee development	Determine elasticity of demand for various services. Consider value of service to clients and assess competitive fees.	Approaches fee development from a cost-plus perspective.
9. Practice development program	Based on a strategic analysis of both needs of firm and diverse needs of targeted client segments.	Based on traditional practice development lore and personal preferences.
10. Use of personal selling	Delivery staff regularly assesses clients' needs. Promotes to new clients and prospects service offerings of direct benefit to them.	Reluctance among staff to actively sell services.

ORGANIZING YOUR MARKETING EFFORTS

There is a difference between the role of marketing within an organization and the method in which a firm chooses to organize its departments and activities so as to become a market-driven firm. There is no one best way to organizationally achieve the objective of a market-driven firm. How to organize depends on many factors, such as number of employees, array of services offered, the location and number of branch offices, and other such considerations. Larger, more diversified firms may need a director of marketing who helps coordinate and centralize marketing functions. Smaller firms may not have any formal marketing position within the organization, but they could still be market-driven firms. Why is this? Because in marketing a service, achieving a marketing orientation rests more on developing the right organizational culture and shared values than it does on organizational design. Many firms have had large formal marketing departments, sophisticated marketing information systems, and absolutely staggering promotional budgets, yet they were not market-driven firms.

Firms without a marketing orientation are characterized by their lack of customer or client orientation, even though they pride themselves on their product and service quality. Usually, products and services are developed because of cost advantages, economies of scale, technological breakthroughs, or the need to keep personnel employed during slack periods. All of these are important considerations, but pale in comparison to these fundamental, strategically important questions marketing-oriented firms ask themselves: What is the mission of the firm? What industry are we competing within? Are our long-range objectives derived from an analysis of the mission of the firm, our strengths and weaknesses, and the needs of the clients we wish to serve? Are long-range goals self-evident in what we are trying to accomplish and are they truly obtainable? What key organizational values should be instilled in employees? Some examples of firms that possess this type of orientation are the Procter & Gamble Co., IBM, Apple Computer, Inc., McDonald's Corporation, Marriott Corporation, Disney Productions, and American Airlines, Inc. These are some of the exemplary firms listed in the book, *In Search of Excellence*.[1]

The above questions are ones that public accounting firms ought to consider. In every listing of exemplary organizations I have reviewed, not one contained the name of a public accounting firm. In fact, the organizational category of professional service suppliers is generally absent from the sampling frame. This is understandable when one considers the reluctance that many professional service suppliers would have to being scrutinized and then openly compared with other organizations competing in different arenas. However, a 1974 study by George and Barksdale indicated that professional service firms were not as marketing-oriented as goods manufacturers. Fragmentation of marketing activities in service firms also held true for all components of the marketing mix.² As the authors of this study point out, "In every case fewer service firms than product firms performed these activities in the marketing department. Furthermore, for the majority of the offering activities, service firms were more likely than product companies to indicate that they did not perform the specific activity." Personal experience in consulting with public accounting firms allows me to believe that the major conclusions of this 1974 study are still generalizable to today's competitive environment.

However, the question that needs to be posed is whether partners and managers within your own firm have addressed this fundamental marketing question: What do our customers desire in a public accounting firm, and how are we satisfying these existing needs? A firm cannot be market-driven if the development of new products or services is based primarily on production and technological and financial considerations rather than on satisfying the researched needs and wants of their customers. When firms lack a true marketing orientation, then marketing's primary, and sometimes sole, function is to sell what was produced.

A classic example of this is the American automobile manufacturers of the 1960s who doggedly continued to produce larger, more expensive automobiles than foreign importers. Daily, consumers were casting their economic vote in favor of smaller cars. However, profit margins were greater with the larger cars, without incurring expensive plant retooling costs. This is a classic example of a production orientation. In fact, the American automobile industry did not produce a smaller car comparable to the imports in wheelbase, size, and price until market pressure forced them to do so in 1971. This was the year the American subcompacts were developed, yet by this time foreign imports had captured the lion's share of the smaller car market. Detroit had formalized marketing departments, sophisticated marketing information systems, and huge promotional budgets. Yet, they were not able to bend demand to the will of supply.

Organizational design is not a guarantee of any one particular type of orientation, merely an indication. I have consulted with several public accounting firms that have created a director of marketing position and in a few cases a marketing department. Some of these firms lacked a true marketing orientation because in their organizational climates marketing continued to mean different things to different people. Many employees believed that marketing was the responsibility of the director of marketing who performed mundane promotional tasks, such as writing a monthly newsletter, developing firm brochures, and engaging in highly visible public relation activities. Staff accountants believed their job was to be technically proficient in performing the commissioned service, while being cordial to clients.

In conclusion, there is a simple, basic, and highly predictive adage to remember. If one wishes to determine what organizations truly value, then look at the activities they engage in, the decisions they make, and what they considered in arriving at these decisions. (This is what George and Barksdale did.) This will generally be a very revealing assessment of the real orientation of the firm. Remember, marketing is a business function a firm has to perform, as well as an orientation (organizational value) to achieve. The purpose of marketing is to help steer the course of the firm and in a sense to plan the obsolescence of the services that presently sustain the very livelihood of the firm. For as Theodore Levitt stated over two decades ago in his classic article "Marketing Myopia," "There is no such thing as a growth industry, only growth opportunities," which a true marketing orientation helps a firm to attain.[3]

Characteristics of Successful Organizations

Hundreds of textbooks and articles have been published in an attempt to determine what makes business firms a success or a failure. Does anybody really have the answer to the question of what makes a firm successful? No, not in any guaranteed sense. However, there has been enough replication among the better studies to allow scholars to identify the characteristics of successful firms. It is important to remember that management is an art, and failure can be attributed to poor execution, an ineffective organizational design, the relationship between the two, or other factors. This added complication makes much more difficult the research task of determining what makes some organizations effective and others failures. No doubt you experience these same vagaries when advising your own clients, but as most business advisors quickly learn, there are no guarantees.

With that point in mind, let's take a look at one study that replicated the findings of earlier studies. Clark's study attempted to determine what makes an organization successful, as well as what some of the causes of failure are. He accomplished this by studying the activities of successful and unsuccessful manufacturing and service organizations. His suppositions concerning success were the following:

1. An aggressive leader who instilled enthusiasm and confidence in employees.
2. An operationally clear mission statement and a general agreement among employees concerning how to accomplish this.
3. A bias toward action or an ability to capitalize on expansion opportunities.
4. The ability to anticipate and respond to changes in external environments, such as legal, social, or environmental influences.
5. A well-thought-out strategic plan.

These findings relate to the management of public accounting firms as much as they do to manufacturing organizations.

On the other hand, what were some of the causes of failure according to Clark's study? There are many, but let's discuss some of the most important ones.

1. An inability to adjust to changing times and evolving consumer needs.
2. Implementing a radical change too late and only half-heartedly.
3. An ineffective positioning of the firm in the marketplace due to a failure to conceptualize company strengths and weaknesses.
4. An inability or reluctance to establish a positive image for the organization.
5. A poor execution of marketing, production, or financial strategies.[4]

Now, let's take a look at the eight attributes Peters and Waterman noted in In Search of Excellence as being distinguishing characteristics of excellent companies. Table 2–2 contains these attributes, which they dubbed a "brilliance on the basics." This listing illustrates a strong relationship between the two studies. What emerges is the proposition that while many excellent firms are competing in different markets, they are alike in the way they run their businesses.

Yet a common belief among professional service suppliers, including public accountants, is that their practices are somehow unique enough that the aforementioned suppositions do not apply. The excellent public accounting firms I have advised, both large

TABLE 2-2

Eight Attributes of Excellent Corporations

1. **A bias for action**—managers who get things done while still retaining their analytical prowess.
2. **Close to the customer**—managers and employees alike listen to their customers. They learn from those whose business they seek to retain.
3. **Autonomy and entrepreneurship**—the values of the organization support practical risk taking and good tries. Employees are not held on such a short rein that creativity and entrepreneurship are stifled.
4. **Productivity through people**—a belief by managers that growth and product or service quality come from people rather than production processes.
5. **Hands on value driven**—organizational values are evident to all. There are no secrets in terms of what the organization values, and reward systems are developed to reinforce these values.
6. **Stick to the knitting**—managers learn to stick to the business (product/ service offerings and customers) they know best.
7. **Simple form, lean staff**—managers keep a staff from proliferating to the extent that bureaucracies develop, empires emerge, and accountability is lost.
8. **Simultaneous loose-tight properties**—managers reward and almost fanatically reinforce basic organizational values while providing employees and departments autonomy in operations.

Source: Based on the book by Thomas J. Peters and Robert H. Waterman, Jr., *In Search of Excellence, Lessons from America's Best-Run Companies* (New York: Harper & Row, 1982).

and small, tended to possess many of the characteristics listed in the studies. I believe that this "brilliance on the basics" that Peters and Waterman describe is largely the cause of the organizational success of these firms. I have noticed these characteristics in other areas of consulting also, and I believe that to make marketing truly work for larger firms most if not all of these attributes have to be present. That is one of the reasons why there is no one way to organize, and why creating a responsive organization, which evolves into a market-driven firm, requires specific organizational steps. Therefore, let's now discuss what to consider when creating a market-driven firm.

Creating a Market-driven Public Accounting Practice

A reoccurring theme of this chapter is that a true marketing orientation is more reliant on the system within the organization than on any specific organizational design. Therefore, creating a responsive organization can be achieved with a variety of organizational formats. For example, creating a formal position within the firm, such as a director of marketing, is one option. A firm can also become a marketing-oriented company without any formal marketing position per se. In such a case, marketing activities are decentralized among existing staff; however, the complication of knowing what to do, how to do it, as well as of coordinating implicit problems among staff is a very real limitation of this approach. Remember that one can eliminate a position, but not the function. This is a real trap to avoid at all costs.

In summary, management has flexibility in selecting an organizational design, but certain organizational prerequisites have to be present in order to make a firm a responsive organization. What does it mean to be a responsive organization? Being a **responsive organization** means operationalizing the marketing concept to the extent that the delivery personnel, not just management or marketing specialists, make a concerted effort to satisfy the needs of both the firm and clients. Obviously, what we are discussing is organizational values, and these values in large part both cause and reinforce a particular orientation within a firm.

Let's now consider six key factors influencing whether or not your own firm can evolve into or maintain a marketing orientation.

1. The Orientation of Key Decision Makers within the Firm. When one studies the earlier works of management scholars (e.g. Leavitt and McKinsey), the wisdom of and need to create shared organizational values is well supported. Organizational values generally originate from top management leaders who are specifically able to establish and reinforce or extinguish a value system.

Therefore, it is very unlikely that a public accounting firm can evolve into a marketing-oriented firm if these leaders, especially the managing partner, are not sure of what marketing really entails, or if they believe that marketing a practice is unprofessional. Others in the organization may feel quite differently, but they may neither possess the direct power or status to change the views of their superiors.

Larger public accounting firms are traditionally conservative, highly structured organizations with many expected, although unwritten, rules to follow. Violate the rules too often, and the chance to move from staff to partner is lessened. In the smaller firms organizational mores are also evident, and the need to "fit-in" is also great. It is therefore imperative that management communicate to staff the importance of marketing, as well as the expectation that specific, defined duties have to be performed by delivery staff and management alike. Performance of these duties has to be built into the reward system if one hopes to change behavior. Failure to do this means that an organization will not be able to evolve into a marketing-oriented firm.

Consider this example. Several years ago I was asked by the marketing manager of a large regional firm to develop for all delivery staff a two day in-house training program. The course was carefully designed so that the end objective was to acquaint the staff with particular marketing duties they should be performing and to develop their sales skills. At the end of the second day, the managing partner, who had previously expressed little interest in the course, attended the last two-hour session. It was very apparent that the marketing orientation I was trying to instill in the staff was bothersome to him. His concern appeared to focus on his perception of the "professionalism" of openly marketing a practice and with the need for staff to more aggressively sell their services. He believed that service quality alone was enough to retain clients. If the client was assured of technical service quality, he argued, then that was proof that the firm was meeting client needs. Unfortunately, I was unable to change his beliefs in the last few hours of the course. Two years later I again met the marketing manager. He told me that morale in the firm was low, staff turnover was high, and there seemed to be great reluctance to depart from the traditional practice development lore the managing partner advocated.

The moral to this story is that even if a staff wishes to become more marketing-oriented, the performance evaluation system has to support this orientation. The old adage of define what you wish to measure, evaluate performance, and reward accomplishments is very true. In highly structured, conservative environments, most professionals will not violate the wishes of the CEO and assume the role of a change agent—and expect to survive and prosper. Without top management's support, the task of turning a production-oriented company into a market-driven firm is next to impossible to accomplish.

2. Incorporate Marketing into the Firm's Training Program. Consider for a moment what marketing means to the professionals working in your own firm. More than likely a specific, shared definition will not come to mind. Also, your staff may not be aware of the types of duties they should be performing in order to execute a marketing strategy. There may also be a philosophical conviction that marketing is not their job or that it is unprofessional to overtly market a practice. These beliefs will not go away, but they will have an impact on practice development efforts, even if they are not frequently articulated.

In-house training is the answer to these problems, because what you are trying to accomplish is to change organizational values. If you want people to change their behavior, then you have to first stipulate what you want them to do. Second, you have to make them want to do it, or they will find their own ways of circumventing your wishes. Last, you have to reward the behavior you wish to reinforce. However, don't fall into the trap of punishing those that have not been successful, or you will stifle the initiative of others. Remember, we learn through our failures as well as our successes. As long as the effort was practical, genuine, and reasonable, then it should be positively acknowledged as a good try.

When developing the in-house training program, it will be necessary to divide the staff into separate groups to more specifically address individual needs. For example, the needs of top management will concern such topics as (1) what to consider when conducting an audit of the firm's resources, (2) how to identify the company's present managerial orientation, (3) how to assess present areas of service specialization, (4) what to consider in the process of creating a marketing plan, and (5) how to identify ways to segment a practice into client/service segments. When meeting with staff, it will be necessary to address the tactical execution of specific duties that have to be performed, as well as to convince them of the need for staff to be actively involved in marketing the practice. It will also be necessary to bring both groups together to show top management's support and to facilitate team building, a very important outcome to attain.

Why am I advocating in-house training versus sending one or two staff members to a CPE course? There are several reasons. First, in-house training can be specifically fitted to the needs and concerns of the firm. Also, it may be less expensive to train in-house than it would be to send several individuals to a training seminar at some distant destination. Too, staff members feel more able to address specific organizational problems and ask for advice at an in-house course than in a room full of competitors. Last, in-house training gives all people the same lexicon, orientation, and shared purpose. Without this training you are operating under the premise that the person who attended the outside course will be able to tell the staff what needs to be done and will be a powerful enough change agent to execute change. I am not opposed to attending outside seminars. They can be very worthwhile, but the orientation is not one of team building. Often it is only possible to address strategy (what to do), rather than strategy and tactics (what to do and how to do it). Whichever approach your firm is able to take, it is necessary to learn from a professional with experience in the field.

3. Consider Marketing Acumen When Hiring New Employees. When hiring new employees, consider their ability to relate to clients' needs and their willingness to help in marketing the practice, as well as their technical prowess. Is there some particular personality profile to seek in applicants? Not really. Rather, you should look for people who have the ability to learn, are articulate enough to influence the decisions of others, and yet are empathetic to the needs and divergent personalities of clients and staff alike. In essence you need professionals who possess some of the attributes of successful salespeople.

However, remember there is no such thing as a sales personality or a typical salesperson, despite stereotyped profiles that exist in our culture. Research clearly shows that while successful salespeople have specific attributes—such as high intelligence, empathy, product or service knowledge, analytical reasoning, and high oral communication skills—there is no one personality type that solely possesses these attributes. Of key consideration is the applicant's willingness to learn, because effective, articulate, sales-oriented people can be developed. They are not just born and naturally evolve into proficiency. Rather one's professional progression is attributed to personal attributes, a willingness to learn, and personal experiences.

When training new staff, be sure to make it clear that they are expected to be an integral part of the marketing of the practice. It may also be necessary to train staff in terms of how to qualify clients' needs, answer clients' objections, refine their own listening skills, and other such responsibilities.

4. Decentralize Marketing Duties. The point has already been made that marketing is not something that the director of marketing does while others perform the technical service. Nor is marketing the sole responsibility of partners. All delivery personnel who come in contact with clients have to be involved in some aspect of marketing. Remember, staff is often viewed by clients in a surrogate capacity for service quality. The value of a technical service may be very difficult for clients to assess, but it is far easier for them to assess delivery personnel. This means that each employee involved with the client, from the receptionist to seniors to partners, will all have particular duties to perform.

These duties will overlap, as would be expected, but each will also have specific responsibilities. The receptionist is responsible for greeting the client and making that person feel welcomed, confirming the appointment, and even in some instances determining the purpose of the visit. Staff accountants, such as seniors, have to assess client needs and present beneficial service offerings to the client as they see a need arise. They are also responsible for explaining in a lucid manner the implicit benefits of certain services, rather than solely discussing service features. The partner or manager in charge of the engagement has a similar responsibility, but he has the added task of assessing if the completed service was consistent with the client's expectations. Additionally, all employees who are involved with the execution of the service should be alert to spotting news items and technological developments that would have an impact on the services the client needs.

Obviously, a marketing manager cannot perform all of these duties. In fact, marketing managers for public accounting firms frequently do not actually perform the technical service. This is why marketing responsibilities have to be decentralized, although there can be a marketing manager who is responsible for long-range planning, staff training, developing the marketing plan, and other such strategic responsibilities. This means that management in the firm has to specify the marketing duties specific personnel have to perform.

There is no short cutting around this basic responsibility. Whether or not management wants to decentralize marketing is not the issue, because in professional service firms marketing will be decentralized if it is to be effective. Therefore, it is imperative not only to stipulate specific duties but also, as previously emphasized, to train people to perform these duties. The performance evaluation system has also to assess to what extent employees collectively, as well as individually, have been performing the stipulated tasks.

In summary, management must develop and support the value system, communicate the expectation, measure the results, and reward performance. Eliminate any of these responsibilities, and the marketing orientation that top management espouses becomes just a nonreinforced value, and we all know what happens to these in an organization!

5. Establish Both Direct and Indirect Rewards. Certainly, employees do not have to be rewarded every time they do something right. Nor do rewards always have to be of a monetary nature such as a bonus, merit raise, or finder fee. Actually, a great deal of our behavior is based on our need for esteem. People want to be appreciated and valued for their contribution to the organization. The organization as a legal entity may mean little to some employees, but one's relationships with fellow employees usually means much more. There are numerous ways perceptive managers can express their satisfaction with the job employees are doing. What is needed first is the realization that such an orientation is important to achieve.

Let's consider this example in illustrating the value of nonmonetary rewards. A management consulting firm I once worked for developed a monetary incentive designed to stimulate referrals. Employees who referred a business prospect to the firm that year received a 10 percent bonus versus the traditional finder fee of 5 percent of first year revenue. Did the program work well? No, it did not because most of the professionals who referred clients did so for reasons other than the finder fee. Yes, the fee was a nice way of making more tangible the appreciation for the referral, but not one additional engagement resulted from the 5 percent increment. Yet, I once consulted with a public accounting firm that did not offer any finder fee to employees for direct referrals. In this company the employees went out of their way to secure leads and give referrals to the partners in charge of the respective division. Why did it happen this way? It was because employees' efforts were noticed, appreciated, rewarded, and, yes, expected. This was a part of their job, and management showed their appreciation in many ways such as tickets to ball games, arranging for a Friday off work, and just expressing appreciation for a job well done. When management's appreciation is real, and can be made tangible in the minds of employees through both monetary and nonmonetary incentives, then often employees' efforts increase markedly.

6. Think Strategically.   A strategy is essentially a determination of what to do, whereas a tactic is how to do something. As the Boston Consulting Group and the PIMS study (a study describing the relationship between profit impact and market share) determined, good strategy development is more important to the profitable operation of a business than any other single element.[5] As discussed in Chapter 1, a marketing strategy is a marketing mix aimed at one or more market segments. Before selecting a specific strategy, management must determine the needs of specific client segments, assess the needs of the firm and possible delivery systems, and then formulate a program incorporating all marketing mix elements (product, price, place, and promotion). Most public accounting firms have been somewhat conditioned to think tactically first.

Consider this example of the difference between a strategic perspective versus a tactical orientation. A CPA firm decides to finally publish their own quarterly client newsletter because other firms have one, and management believes they should as well. In this example this firm is developing a promotional/informational service based on what? This is merely a tactical decision to do something. A strategic perspective would first identify which clients the firm ought to reach, what ought to be communicated, the frequency needed, and then compare alternative delivery systems. The development of the newsletter would ultimately be evaluated in terms of how it fits into the overall marketing strategy. Remember, it is important to think first strategically, because often corporate fortunes are based on simple but fundamental decisions of a strategic nature. We will examine closely several strategic alternatives public accounting firms ought to consider in Chapter 5.

NOTES

1. Thomas J. Peters and Robert H. Waterman, Jr., *In Search of Excellence, Lessons from America's Best-Run Companies* (New York: Harper & Row, 1982).
2. William R. George and Hiram C. Barksdale, "Marketing Activities in the Service Industries," *Journal of Marketing*, October 1974, pp. 65–70.
3. Theodore Levitt, "Marketing Myopia," *Harvard Business Review*, July–August 1960.
4. John Clark, *Business Today: Successes and Failures* (New York: Random House, 1979).
5. For a more detailed discussion of strategic planning refer to the following references: Sidney Schoeffler, Robert D. Buzzell, and Donald F. Hearny, "Impact of Strategic Planning on Profit Performance," *Harvard Business Review*, March–April 1974, pp. 137–45; Derek F. Abell and John S. Hammond, *Strategic Market Planning: Problems and Analytical Approaches* (Englewood Cliffs, N.J.: Prentice-Hall, 1979).

Creating an Effective Marketing Information System

"The challenge in creating an effective marketing information system is not in creating a technological marvel. Rather, the challenge is to create a workable system which provides timely, relevant information while avoiding the real trap of drowning users in meaningless data, while starving them for information."

Obtaining marketing information is essential in successfully applying the marketing concept. Public accounting firms must have a systematic and continuous flow of marketing information in order to make informed marketing decisions. Effective management always relies on obtaining timely information about the different environments a firm operates within. This is a requisite for market success because strategic decisions have to be based on information. Without this needed information managers are forced to rely on guesses and intuition, which is a poor substitute for knowledge.

Generally speaking, the more information public accountants have about their target markets, competitors, changes in the business composition of their trading area, and referral sources, the better able they are to develop an effective marketing program. This information also has to be timely; therefore, managers can't wait until a problem develops and then initiate the process of acquiring information. By the time the needed information is compiled, it may be too late to react to the situation. Thus, what is needed is an efficient, continuous means of acquiring marketing information. As the paragraph at the beginning of this chapter indicates, the challenge is to create an effective information system that does not drown users in data while starving them for information.

ESTABLISHING A MARKETING INFORMATION SYSTEM

In order to establish a marketing information system, managers must first identify their need for specific types of information. Later they develop a system for gathering, recording, and periodically analyzing the needed information. What we are talking about is creating a type of "on-line" **marketing information system**, or **MIS**. An MIS is a firm's formal system of gathering, organizing, and reporting information.[1] For larger firms this means a more sophisticated system designed to provide many departmental users with a continuous flow of relevant information. For smaller firms, with fewer users and more centralized decision making, their MIS will not be as elaborate. Therefore, MISs can be useful for all firms, but each public accounting firm must tailor a system to meet its organizational needs and constraints. The capabilities and limitations of such a system are listed in Table 3–1.

The first step in the developmental process is that the firm must determine what kind of information is needed and by whom. Different levels of management have different needs, so the system must be sensitive to the specific needs of all users.

Second, the firm must determine early in the process where and how to acquire the needed information. There are two sources of marketing data, classified as either primary or secondary data sources. As Figure 3–1 indicates, an effective MIS will use both sources. **Primary data** is data generated for a particular and immediate use, such as a questionnaire study concerning clients' satisfaction with firm. **Secondary data** is information previously compiled for some other use, such as information the firm obtained from business directories or from its own files.

Third, management must consider how to incorporate the information into their system, so it is available to users when needed. This will necessitate the following:

TABLE 3-1

Capabilities and Limitations of a Marketing Information System

What an MIS Can Do	What an MIS Cannot Do
1. Track progress toward long-term strategic goals.	1. Replace managerial judgment.
2. Aid in day-to-day decision making.	2. Provide all the information a manager needs to make an infallible decision.
3. Establish a common language between marketing and "back office" operations.	3. Work successfully without management support.
4. Consider the impact of alternative environmental scenarios.	4. Work successfully without management confidence.
5. Automate many labor-intensive data processing activities, thus effecting cost savings.	5. Work successfully without being adequately maintained and responsive to management needs.
6. Serve as an early warning device for portions of a service business that are not on target.	
7. Help determine how to allocate resources to achieve marketing goals.	
8. Deliver condensed, actionable information in a timely and useful manner.	
9. Help service customers.	
10. Allow improvement of overall performance through better planning and control.	

Source: Adapted from Barbara Howard, "Intelligence: How to Build an Effective Marketing Information System," *Marketing Update,* Issue 20 (New York: Alexander-Norton, Inc., 1977), p. 5. Excerpted from Eugene M. Johnson, Eberhard E. Scheuing, and Kathleen A. Gaida, *Profitable Service Marketing* (Homewood: Dow Jones-Irwin, 1986), p. 81.

1. The development of new internal reporting forms on which periodic reports will be based.
2. The assigning of alphanumeric codes to clients and services so billings can be compared from one reporting period to another.
3. The formulation of an indexed filing system for secondary data sources, for example, the filing of reference articles concerning specific service offerings a firm is interested in promoting.
4. Primary data, in the form of marketing research, may also need to be obtained and periodically updated.

FIGURE 3–1

Sources of Secondary and Primary Data

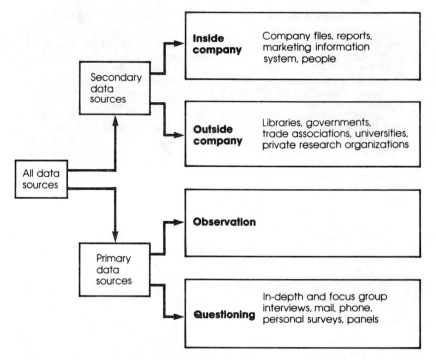

Source: E. Jerome McCarthy and William D. Perreault, Jr., *Basic Marketing,* 8th ed. (Homewood, Ill.: Richard D. Irwin, 1984), p. 145.

Fourth, the actual design of the system, including computer equipment and software, has to be determined. The more expensive main frame computers and customized programs are not always necessary. Micro computers and existing software programs are often all that a firm needs for a basic reporting and processing system. Software programs such as dBASE III® or 1-2-3 from Lotus® can be used for a variety of record keeping and spreadsheet applications.

Finally, management has to convince the staff of the need and uses of a system, and then they must be trained in how to obtain and use the acquired information. Of course, management has to address the issue of maintaining system integrity and limiting access to sensitive pieces of information prior to training the staff. Most MISs will be a failure unless their development and use are supported by the firm's partners and especially the managing partner. Therefore, visible support has to be evident, and, as in all cases, employee use of the system has to be monitored. If employees know they have specific responsibilities and will be evaluated in terms of performance, then they are more likely to engage in the type of behavior desired. Without this visible support, employee apathy towards a system top management is not really excited about may become a problem.

COMPONENTS OF AN MIS

There are three key components of an MIS that should be a part of every system. Each component, as Figure 3–2 indicates, is responsible for generating specific types of information. Collectively, all three components span the marketing informational needs of the firm and work in harmony with each other. Each component, therefore, is similar to a gear in a drive system. Each gear revolves on an independent axle, but it also helps drive the entire system. Let's take a look at each component of this system in order to better conceptualize the types of information that need to be compiled.

FIGURE 3–2

Marketing Information System

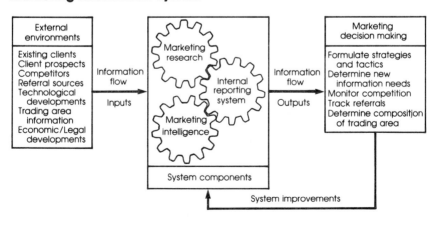

Marketing Research

The first component is marketing research, which generally relies on external information obtained through primary sources such as client surveys. **Marketing research** is the systematic gathering, recording, and analyzing of data about problems relating to the marketing of goods and services.[2] Marketing research generally involves the formal collection and analysis of data for some specific problem facing management. As such, marketing research is a necessary component of a marketing information system. Yet, a common error is to assume that a marketing information system is merely another term for marketing research.[3] There are several key differences between the two, which Table 3–2 illustrates.

TABLE 3–2

Differences between MIS and Marketing Research

Marketing Research	Marketing Information System
1. Emphasis is on handling external information.	1. Handles both internal and external data.
2. Is concerned with solving problems.	2. Is concerned with preventing and solving problems.
3. Operates in a fragmented, intermittent fashion—on a project-to-project basis.	3. Operates continuously—is a system.
4. Tends to focus on past information.	4. Tends to be future-oriented.
5. Need not be computer-based.	5. Is a computer-based process.
6. Is one source of information input for a marketing information system.	6. Includes other subsystems besides marketing research.

Source: William J. Stanton, *Fundamentals of Marketing,* 7th ed. (New York: McGraw-Hill, 1984), p. 47.

Some typical examples of marketing research conducted by public accounting firms are these:

1. Studies designed to assess the image of the firm.
2. An estimation of clients' receptiveness toward new service offerings the firm wishes to develop.
3. The selection of alternative sites for a branch office.
4. The description of target market segments.
5. An analysis of the competitive fee structure in a particular trading area.

Consequently, marketing research is specifically used to furnish answers to research questions when the necessary information cannot be readily determined from internal reports or existing secondary sources, such as periodical articles or census data. However, as Figure 3–3 indicates, there are distinct stages of the research project, and at any stage an error can occur.[4]

The more complicated marketing research studies should be directed by professionals who have the necessary training and experience. An example of a study for which you generally need to obtain technical assistance is one that you are trying to assess the image of your firm. Yet, there are situations, such as selecting the location for a new branch office or determining clients' satisfaction with service quality, that public accountants can engage in this form of research with little or no technical assistance. There are, however, too many situations where a poorly developed questionnaire is sent to clients or referral sources. If the research problem statement is unclear to management, subsequent problems in the wording of questions, the development of valid measurement scales, the selection of the sample, and the statistical analysis of the data generally prevail. These problems remain undetected, and numerical findings are viewed as being valid simply because they appear to be so exacting. A case in point further illustrates this problem.

A Michigan public accounting firm was losing clients to several more aggressive competitors. The managing partner believed the firm had an "image problem," so he developed a brief questionnaire designed to assess the firm's image. Partners and managers alike were asked to submit the names of 10 clients they thought would truthfully respond to the questionnaire. The firm did not wish to overly dramatize the problem by surveying all clients, so only 40 clients were selected. Twenty-five questionnaires were returned. What did the study reveal? Thirteen of the clients indicated that the fees the firm charged were perceived as being high. Some partners believed that this perception might be causing the firm to have a high-priced image. Therefore, the planned increase in fees was summarily abandoned, and fees were locked-in for two years at the existing rate.

Unfortunately, the study was ill-conceived and poorly executed, and the interpretation of the findings was mostly conjectural. Both the number and type of clients surveyed did not represent the firm's client profile. The sample contained a disproportionate number of smaller tax clients and retailers. Also, in general the questions were poorly worded. Of course the less affluent clients were more price sensitive to begin with. Too, the questionnaire never asked whether the client was a new or old client, an experienced

FIGURE 3–3

Decision Points in a Marketing Research Project

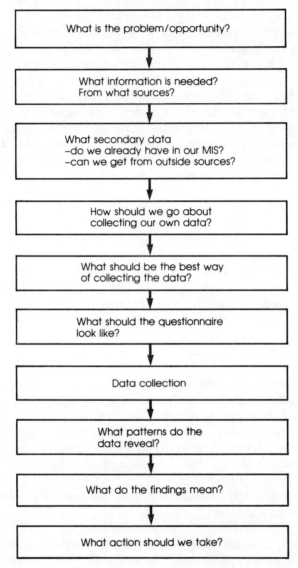

Source: Eugene M. Johnson, Eberhard E. Scheuing, and Kathleen A. Gaida, *Profitable Service Marketing* (Homewood, III.: Dow Jones-Irwin, 1986), p. 90.

consumer of accounting services, or a neophyte. All responses counted equally, and yet the respondents all had different points of reference. In fact, a better conceived and executed study three years later found out that a large percentage of this firm's clients, in general, felt that the fees public accountants, attorneys, and physicians charged were too high! Yet questions pertaining to the firm's service quality indicated that the majority of clients were highly satisfied.

Unfortunately, thousands of dollars in revenue were lost due to the ill-conceived and poorly executed study. The moral to this story is not to shoot yourself in the foot by gathering and interpreting misleading information. Technical assistance can be obtained from marketing professors at nearby universities or colleges, from marketing research firms, marketing consultants, and other such research specialists. These individuals can be very valuable in objectively helping you formulate the research problem, design data-gathering instruments, select the sample, and statistically analyze and interpret the findings.

Internal Reporting System

Another key component of a MIS for public accounting firms is the **internal reporting system.** The basic function of this component of an MIS is to provide continuous feedback concerning the success of the firm's marketing effort. Some examples of the types of reports that are an output of an internal reporting component of an MIS are as follows:

1. Quarterly fee reports that summarize billings by service and type of client. Data from previous quarters and past years can be invaluable in helping managers estimate and react to changes in demand.
2. Periodic summaries of the number of new clients obtained, the number lost and the reasons for the attrition, as well as the number of prospect inquiries received.
3. Increases or decreases in categorized service offerings, (tax, auditing, write-up work, etc.) compared to the preceeding base period.
4. The increase in dollar billings from new services sold to existing clients organized by employee number and/or division of the firm. Again, period comparisons can be quite revealing.
5. Periodic, summary tabulations of brief postservice evaluation forms filled out by clients. A categorized, numerical

breakdown of the reasons for being satisfied or dissatisfied with the service is quite helpful in determining corrective measures.

Marketing Intelligence

The third and last necessary component of a MIS is the **marketing intelligence system**. The basic function of this component is to report changes in the external environment so that a firm can react to these developments. Some examples of the types of information that need to be systematically obtained and periodically reported are the following:

1. *Competitive information.* Employees must be trained to fill out **competitive activity reports** that provide information about changes in principal competitors' marketing mix activities. Changes in service offerings, fee schedules, promotional programs, the acquisition of major new clients, branch office expansions, and like developments are the type of information that needs to be compiled. See Figure 3–4. This information is then added to the system as it is acquired.

2. *Prospect files.* Employees should be alert to recording organizational and financial information about prospective clients that a firm would like to engage. Of course, the first step is to target select clients, alert employees to look for the types of information needed, and then develop some type of reporting system, such as the brief form contained in Figure 3–5. If a firm wishes to develop a master prospect list for a larger geographical area, such as a state or region, then list brokers should be used. Thousands of lists indexed by Standard Industrial Classification (SIC) number, or type of business activity, (e.g. state banks) are available from list brokers and compilers for as little as $50 for 1,000 names. Financial and organizational information about key prospects can then be obtained from such secondary publications as *Moody's Industrial Manual, Dun & Bradstreet Middle Market Directory,* or *Fairchild's Financial Manual of Retail Stores.*

3. *Industrial composition of the market.* Information needs to be compiled that delineates the number of business firms within a trading area categorized by size of firm (sales if possible), type of business activity, products/services produced, and number of employees. Fortunately, a great deal of this information can be obtained from U.S. Department of Commerce, *County Business Patterns, Dunn's Census of American Business,* annual reports, as well as periodicals. The use of *County Business Patterns* will be

FIGURE 3-4

Competitor Data Form

Firm name: _____

Address of main office: _____

Location of branch offices: _____   _____

_____   _____   _____

Number of employees: _____

Estimated yearly billings: _____

Do we directly compete against this firm? _____ Yes   _____ No

Strongest service offerings: _____   _____

_____   _____

_____   _____

_____   _____

Client mix:

_____

_____

_____

_____

_____

Reputation/Image of firm:

_____

_____

_____

_____

_____

Fee structure:

_____

_____

Promotional emphasis:

_____

_____

_____

_____

Describe any areas of specialization:

_____

_____

_____

_____

FIGURE 3-5

Prospect Data Form

Name of company or prospect: _____

Business address: _____

_____

Telephone: (_____) _____

SIC code: / Type of business: _____   _____

Products/Services produced: _____

_____

_____

_____

Annual sales: _____

Credit rating/financial condition: _____

Number of employees: _____

Contact person(s):

Name	Position
_____	_____
_____	_____
_____	_____

Anticipated service needs: _____

_____

Accounting firm presently used: _____

Please rate this prospect's development potential:

_____

_____

_____

Contact Record

Employee	Contact person	Results of contact
1. _____	_____	_____
2. _____	_____	_____
3. _____	_____	_____

Indicate possible referral service: _____

discussed later in this chapter since this is a particularly useful source of information.

4. *Referral sources.* It is necessary to identify likely referral sources, as well as try to determine which individuals actually send specific clients to your firm. This helps a firm in refining its professional networking activities. This is not as difficult a task as it may first seem. Employees have to learn to ask new clients how they came to select your firm over others. If the client was sent by some referral source, then a personalized thank you letter should be sent to that person, or a member of the firm should telephone and express his or her thanks directly. Each likely referral agent should have a separate data form on which referral activity and follow up action can be recorded. Obviously, as new referral sources surface, then they should be added to the list, while unproductive sources are deleted. Annually, a brief report of referral activity, based on these tracking forms, should be openly discussed with the partners of the firm. This will help management in refining their referral development program.

5. *Technological, economic, and legal developments affecting clients' demand for services.* How does one possibly gather, organize, and file such voluminous information to be used at some later date? It is a difficult task at best, but not impossible. A filing system organized by subject matter (such as accounting software, inventory control, compensation plans, lease/buy evaluations, etc.) needs to be developed and used by staff. When employees read technical journals and periodicals, they should be alert to saving information that would be of value to existing or prospective clients. That information needs to be filed under the appropriate title, so other members of the firm can use this information as the need arises.

For example, a partner of the firm knows that a solvent, but aging, farm client has a temporary liquidity problem and is in need of a new harvester to replace his damaged, old one. There are also cash flow problems, taxation considerations, and estate planning issues that need to be considered prior to purchasing or leasing equipment. The need for a lease/buy study is clearly warranted. However, the benefits and complexity of this service are not evident to the client, who hastily rejects the need for this service. In an attempt to inform this unsophisticated client about the benefits of lease/buy studies, the partner in charge of the engagement refers to the files. He is in luck because he finds a very straightforward article that clearly describes the benefits of this service and raises some important considerations. He then sends the article to the client along with a brief note explaining that the service benefits described in the article pertain to this client's situation.

This may sound like a farfetched example, but I have worked with public accounting firms that used technical information in exactly this manner. The challenge is to train the staff to responsibly add to the files, use them wisely, and not be guilty of merely adding to file clutter. A lot of this information can be obtained as needed from libraries, and at times this will be necessary. Yet, staff are more likely to refer to in-house sources than engage in a literature search at the local library.

USING SECONDARY SOURCES OF INFORMATION

Secondary sources of information can be invaluable aids in your practice development efforts. There is a wealth of specific information available that many public accountants fail to use. This is truly unfortunate because secondary sources of information can help answer very important questions such as the following:

1. How many businesses of a certain type (e.g. truck leasing firms) are located within the county or state I compete within?

2. What are the relative sizes of these firms in terms of either sales, number of employees, or both? Who are the major officers of these organizations?

3. How do I determine the business composition of county A versus county B, so as to intelligently select the most promising location for a branch office? What is the business composition of the counties I am presently competing within?

4. How do I determine names, addresses, and contact representatives for all potential advertising media within my trading area?

5. How do I obtain financial information about a firm, such as a long-term record of earnings, principal plants and subsidiaries, and product lines without directly contacting the firm?

6. Where can I obtain the names and addresses of different list brokers or compilers who could provide me with a listing of specific types of organizations (e.g. physicians) residing within my state, county, or city.

7. How do I determine the names and addresses of industrial and trade associations servicing a particular type of industry?

Answers to these and many other similar questions can be obtained by using the sources annotated in the appendix at the end of this chapter. In fact specific guides describing these and many other secondary sources are available for your use in the larger libraries. A secondary data guide of particular interest is *Encyclopedia of Business Information Sources*, (Detroit: Gale Research Company). This guide describes the types and sources of information available on a wide variety of business subjects, including statistical sources, periodicals, directories, handbooks, associations, and general literature. Guides such as these, and there are many of them, quickly help you in identifying where you can find the information you need to compile before making informed marketing decisions.

Another source of particular interest to public accountants is *County Business Patterns (CBP)*. This is published annually for each state, as well as the United States as a whole. This series, which is organized by SIC codes, covers virtually every economic sector of the economy from agriculture to industry to trade to services.[5]

Table 3–3 contains an excerpt of a *CBP* report. These reports are specifically helpful in conceptualizing the business composition of a geographical area and comparing possible locations for a branch office. In fact *CBP* contains data on some economic activities not covered in the economic census the U.S. Census Bureau conducts every five years. These include banking, real estate, and insurance. You can obtain *County Business Patterns* reports for a nominal fee from the U.S. Government Printing Office. Flexible diskettes, microfiche, and computer tapes are also available from Customer Services (DUSD), Bureau of the Census, Washington, DC 20233.

NOTES

1. Eugene M. Johnson, Eberhard E. Scheuing, and Kathleen A. Gaida, *Profitable Service Marketing* (Homewood, Ill.: Dow Jones-Irwin, 1986), p. 81.

2. *Report of Definitions Committee of the American Marketing Association* (Chicago, Ill.: American Marketing Association, 1961).

3. William J. Stanton, *Fundamentals of Marketing*, 7th ed. (New York: McGraw-Hill, 1984), p. 47.

4. Johnson et al., *Profitable Service Marketing*, p. 90.

5. For more information concerning how to use *County Business Patterns* see *Economic Data Product Primer #13, County Business Patterns* (Washington, D.C.: U.S. Department of Commerce, Bureau of the Census, April, 1986), p. 1.

TABLE 3-3

County Business Patterns, CBP-83, Kansas

SIC Code	Industry	Number of Employees for Week Including March 12	Payroll ($1,000)		Number of Establishments, by Employment-Size Class									
			First Quarter	Annual	Total	1 to 4	5 to 9	10 to 19	20 to 49	50 to 99	100 to 249	250 to 499	500 to 999	1,000 or More
	Woodson Total	608	1,413	6,038	126	88	26	7	4	1	—	—	—	—
	Mining	107	291	1,208	27	16	10	1	—	—	—	—	—	—
13	Oil and gas extraction	107	291	1,208	27	16	10	1	—	—	—	—	—	—
138	Oil and gas field services	58	177	716	16	11	4	1	—	—	—	—	—	—
	Contract construction	18	43	201	7	5	2	—	—	—	—	—	—	—
	Manufacturing	(B)	(D)	(D)	3	—	2	1	—	—	—	—	—	—
23	Apparel and other textile products	(B)	(D)	(D)	1	—	—	1	—	—	—	—	—	—
232	Men's and boys' furnishings	(B)	(D)	(D)	1	—	—	1	—	—	—	—	—	—
2,321	Men's and boys' shirts and nightwear	(B)	(D)	(D)	1	—	—	1	—	—	—	—	—	—
	Transportation and other public utilities	33	141	583	7	4	2	—	—	1	—	—	—	—
	Wholesale trade	47	141	594	11	7	3	1	—	—	—	—	—	—
	Retail trade	137	194	850	34	27	3	3	1	—	—	—	—	—
58	Eating and drinking places	66	53	249	8	5	—	2	1	—	—	—	—	—
5,812	Eating places	(B)	(D)	(D)	7	4	—	2	1	—	—	—	—	—
	Finance, insurance, and real estate	42	118	529	6	3	2	—	1	—	—	—	—	—
	Services	127	206	893	21	16	2	1	2	—	—	—	—	—
80	Health services	(B)	(D)	(D)	4	—	1	1	2	—	—	—	—	—
805	Nursing and personal care facilities	(B)	(D)	(D)	2	—	—	—	2	—	—	—	—	—
	Nonclassifiable establishments	(A)	(D)	(D)	10	10	—	—	—	—	—	—	—	—

Note: A: 0–19; B: 20–99; C: 100–249; E: 250–499; F: 500–999; G: 1,000–2,499; H: 2,500–4,999; I: 5,000–9,999; J: 10,000–24,999; K: 25,000–49,999; L: 50,000–99,999; M: 100,000 or more.

Source: Economic Data Project Primer #13, County Business Patterns, U.S. Department of Commerce, Washington, D.C., p. 1.

APPENDIX SOURCES OF SECONDARY DATA

GOVERNMENTAL GUIDES

Census of Agriculture. Taken every five years; provides detailed breakdowns by state and county on the number of farms, farm types, acreage, land use practices, employment, livestock produced and products raised, and value of products.

County Business Patterns. An annual publication that contains statistics on the number of businesses by type and their employment and payroll broken down by county.

County and City Data Book. Published every five years by the Bureau of the Census. Provides breakdowns on a city and county basis and includes statistics on population, education, employment, income, housing, banking, manufacturing output and capital expenditures, retail and wholesale sales, and mineral and agricultural output.

Census of Government. Taken every five years; contains information on state and local governments, including employment, size of payroll, amount of indebtedness, and operating revenues and costs.

Census of Manufacturers. Taken every five years; categorizes manufacturing establishments by type. Contains detailed industry and geographic statistics for such items as the number of establishments, quantity of output, value added in manufacture, employment, wages, inventories, sales by customer class. The *Annual Survey of Manufacturers* covers the years between publications of the census.

Census of Retail Trade. Taken every five years; contains detailed statistics on retail stores classified by type of business. Statistics are presented on such things as the number of stores, total sales, and employment. The statistics are reported by counties, cities, and standard metropolitan statistical areas.

State and Metropolitan Area Data Book. A statistical abstract supplement of the Department of Commerce; contains information on population, housing, government, manufacturing, retail and wholesale trade, and some services by state and standard metropolitan statistical areas.

Census of Service Industries.   Taken every five years; provides data on receipts, employment, type of business, and number of units by geographical area.

Census of Wholesale Trade.   Taken every five years; classifies wholesalers into over 150 business groups. It contains statistics on functions wholesalers perform, sales volume, warehouse space, and expenses. Also, it presents these statistics for counties, cities, and standard metropolitan statistical areas.

PRIVATE GUIDES

Almanac of Business and Industrial Financial Ratios.   This annual Prentice-Hall publication contains number of establishments, sales, and some operating ratios for selected industries. Data are supplied by the Internal Revenue Service and allow the comparison of a particular company's financial ratios with competitors of similar size.

Dun & Bradstreet Million Dollar and Middle Market Directory. Published annually by Dun & Bradstreet; lists the offices, products, sales, and number of employees by company. Volume I contains this information for companies with a total worth of more than $1 million while Volume II contains the same information for companies with assets of $500,000 to $999,999.

Editor and Publisher Market Guide.   Published annually by *Editor and Publisher* magazine; contains data on 1,500 United States and Canadian cities, including location, population, number of households, principal industries, retail sales and outlets, and climate.

Encyclopedia of Associations.   Published by Gale Research Co. This is a three-volume guide to nonprofit associations and similar organizations primarily of national scope in various fields. Lists organizations according to basic types such as trade, business, and commerce groups; chambers of commerce; public affairs organizations; and scientific, engineering, and technical associations. Gives name, headquarters address, year founded, name and title of managing official, number of members and staff, official publication. Alphabetical and key word index.

Fairchild's Financial Manual of Retail Stores. Published by Fairchild Publications, Inc., contains financial information on major publicly owned retail organizations. Manual contains addresses of officers, directors, branches; gives data on capital surplus, income before taxes, earnings, 2-year comparison of assets and liabilities; 10-year comparisons of net sales and profits.

Directory of Mailing List Houses. Published by B. Klein Publications, Inc., it is a guide to mailing list houses in the United States, arranged geographically. Shows name, address, and details types of lists handled and mailing services offered.

Moody's Manuals. These annually published manuals (Banks and Finance, Industrials, Municipals and Governments, Public Utilities, Transportation) contain balance sheet and income statements for individual companies and government units.

R. L. Polk & Co. Compilers of all types of business lists. A catalog of mailing and prospect lists, by kinds and numbers of firms, that shows the price of each such list. It is available free on request.

Poor's Register of Corporations, Directors and Executives. Published annually by Standard and Poor, this register lists officers, products, sales, and employees for some 30,000 United States and Canadian corporations.

Thomas Register of American Manufacturers. Published annually by Thomas Publishing Company. This 10-volume publication lists the specific manufacturers of individual products and provides information on their address, branch offices, and subsidiaries.

Sales Management Survey of Buying Power. Published annually by *Sales Management* magazine; contains market data for states, a number of counties, cities, and standard metropolitan statistical areas. Included are statistics on population, retail sales, and household income, and a combined index of buying power for each reported geographic area.

GUIDES TO SECONDARY DATA SOURCES

Daniels, Lorne M.

Business Information Sources. (Berkeley, Calif.: University of California Press, 1976). A guide to the basic sources of business information organized by subject area.

Encyclopedia of Business Information Sources, 4th ed. (Detroit: Gale Research Company, 1980). A guide to the information available on various subjects, including basic statistical sources, associations, periodicals, directories, handbooks, and general literature.

Frank, Nathalie D.

Market Analysis: A Handbook of Current Data Sources, 2nd ed. (Metuchen, N.J.: Scarecrow Press, 1969). An annotated guide to original statistical sources arranged by source of information rather than by topic.

Understanding Client Behavior

"Organizational buying behavior is a complex process (rather than a single, instantaneous act) and involves many persons, multiple goals, and potentially conflicting decision criteria. It often takes place over an extended period of time, requires information from many sources, and encompasses many interorganizational relationships."

Frederick E. Webster, Jr., and **Yoram Wind**[1]

As the marketing concept implies, satisfying the needs and wants of your clients is the pivotal focus of modern day marketing. If you had perfect knowledge of clients' needs and wants, you would be able, at least in theory, to develop a marketing mix that would perfectly satisfy these needs. But acquiring this information is not always an easy task and actually relies more on what you do than on your clients' behavior. Sometimes it is quite difficult to determine these informational needs because clients do not always know their needs. They may even be reluctant to discuss their problems with you until a position of trust is earned. Additionally, they lack the technical knowledge to identify specific service needs, which may be evident to practicing professionals. Also, consumers of public accounting services are not always able to

55

identify the specific qualifications their public accounting firm ought to possess.

Public accounting firms cannot be all things to all clients. Unlike many goods manufacturers, public accounting firms cannot routinize their production process and standardized their methods of distribution and promotion in order to benefit as greatly from economies of scale. This means that portions of the aggregate market for public accounting services, called **target markets**, have to be first identified and then cultivated. For it is quite inefficient to continually attempt to service the needs of the entire market. Client segments, who demand select kinds of services, have to be singled out, their needs must be assessed, and then a marketing mix must be targeted toward these segments. This is a crucial and fundamentally important conclusion for your firm to make. Public accountants will be better able to assess client needs and to develop both marketing and technical expertise and operational marketing mixes if they employ this segmentation approach to practice development. The next two chapters will tell you how to do this.

ANALYZING THE BEHAVIOR OF CLIENTS

CPAs, in order to be successful marketers of their services, must develop an appreciation of how present, as well as prospective, clients make decisions. Purchase decisions are based on clients' expectations of benefits. Clients, like household consumers, purchase products and services that provide solutions to their problems. Clients commission services and hire specific public accounting firms based on an assessment of their needs. Their evaluations, like the ones we daily make as consumers, can be either factual assessments or incorrect appraisals. CPAs must therefore be an integral part of this assessment process, even though clients initially determine their needs without the help of professional counsel. Consequently, the task of any professional service supplier is to first identify clients' perceived needs.

Identifying Clients' Needs

It is imperative that CPAs identify clients' needs and openly discuss how the benefits of specific services relate to these needs. This process has to be a highly interactive one between the service supplier and the client. For both differ from each other in how they assess service needs.

For example, consider the client who hires a CPA to prepare a simple Form 1040 and accompanying schedules. The CPA is hired because of the client's perception of needs as well as the expectation of benefits. The client's vocalized needs are convenience (someone else preparing his return) and the need to save money (the expectation that an accountant can reduce tax liability). After an analysis the accountant realizes that this client also needs tax planning so as to further reduce taxes. This new service is openly discussed, and the benefits of developing a financial plan, based in part on taxation considerations, is related back to the client's stated needs.

In the preceding example, the CPA first qualified the client's needs and explained how tax planning met these needs. The specific benefits of this service were then related to the client's expressed needs. Some CPAs have learned this interactive process of analysis, but all too frequently accounting services are still explained from a technical production perspective.

When accountants describe services from a technical production perspective and then quote a fee range, clients are faced with justifying the expenditure. In short, (they have to sell themselves on the value of the service and balance unqualified value in relation to real cost. They are often asked to do this before they are ready to make a purchase commitment. In such a situation it is far easier for the client to reduce risk by failing to make an affirmative decision.

As Figure 4–1 indicates there is a process clients follow before they make a purchase decision. Consider this process in analyzing client behavior, and the chances of successfully securing an engagement will be far greater. Clients' purchase decisions have to be preceded by desire before commitments can be made. Desire is based on the expectation of benefits. Yet, public accountants too frequently tend to discuss technical features of an engagement or dwell on how the service is performed. This is similar to a car salesman telling you how the automobile you expressed an interest in was manufactured. You listen, but unless this explanation conveys specific benefits, you quickly lose interest and start to drift away from an affirmative decision.

In summary, clients base purchase decisions on the benefits derived from an engagement rather than the technical features of the service. They may listen to production-related issues and even exhibit interest, but their purchase decision will be based on their expectation of derived benefits. Technical features, which do not readily convey benefits, are meaningless to most clients. Needs have to be first identified and discussed; then the benefits of a service or of employing your firm versus another have to be pointedly related to these needs. Staff may well have to be trained in

FIGURE 4–1

Stages in Adoption Process

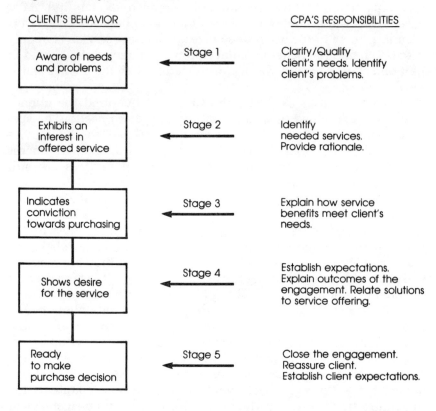

how to uncover client needs and how to relate service benefits to these needs. Helping them understand the behavioral process outlined in Figure 4–1 should be a part of this training.

Identifying Decision Makers and Influence Agents

Frequently when dealing with organizations, more than one person is involved in the decision to hire a firm or commission a service. Each individual has different roles, needs, and different expectations of performance. These individuals also exert varying degrees of influence on the determination of what to do. That is why it is important to identify who exerts particular influence in the decision-making process, and what evaluative criteria each base decisions upon.

For example, a firm's audit committee may have certain prerequisites they have to consider. The office manager may be most concerned with how the audit process will interrupt normal office routine. Top management may be more concerned with the recommendations that relate to specific discussed categories. They all have different needs, and in many instances all these individuals exert varying degrees of influence upon who will be hired as well as retained.

The following is a useful method of categorizing these varying roles.

1. **Key decision makers (KDMs).**   This is generally an individual, but there can be a group of people who make the actual purchase decision. This person (or persons) may not be users of the technical service and may even have different needs, yet he or she makes the purchase decision. Whenever possible, meet with these individuals and assess their needs and determine their expectations.

2. **Gatekeepers.**   These individuals are people who control the flow of information within an organization. For example, an audit committee may request that only invited accounting firms bid on an engagement. No other firm can present its proposal unless approved by this committee.

3. **Users.**   These are people within the organization who will use the information provided by the public accounting firm. Frequently, but not always, they are actively involved in the selection process. They generally have specific service needs that must be identified and then fulfilled in order for them to be satisfied with the engagement. Determine their needs and expectations because present, as well as future, adoption decisions will be based on how they perceive your ability to meet these needs.

4. **Influencing agents.**   These can be individuals either inside the firm or external agents. Influence agents, as their name implies, influence the purchasing decision. For example, bankers can influence the decision concerning which public accounting firm a loan applicant selects to prepare certified financial statements.

5. **Purchasing agents.**   These are members of the organization who have the formal responsibility for identifying competitive suppliers, negotiating terms, and arranging payment conditions. Purchasing agents are more common when dealing with some branches of the federal government and larger, highly centralized organizations.

It is also common for a person or group to assume more than one of these roles. For example, an audit committee could function in the capacity of a gatekeeper and KDM while several, if not all, of its members are users of the service. This would certainly simplify the assessment task for bidding firms. In many cases public accounting firms have direct access to users, but fail to meet with the KDMs and internal influencing agents. Consequently, it is helpful to identify these other individuals and assess their influence in the adoption process.

Factors Influencing the Selection of a CPA Firm

As previously discussed, clients base their adoption decisions on their perceptions of how a specific firm and service meet their needs. However, they do consider other factors as well. Consider your own behavior as a consumer when purchasing a product or service. How something fits your needs is foremost in your mind. Yet, you do consider other factors before arriving at a decision concerning what you are going to purchase and from whom. Table 4–1 lists some of these other factors that consumers of public accounting services consider. A perusal of Table 4–1 indicates that the majority of respondents in each group generally rate the following to be the most important factors to consider in both selecting and evaluating the performance of public accounting firms:

1. Technical competence.
2. Overall reputation of the firm.
3. Quality of the work performed.
4. Experience in the industry.

Two other factors of lesser, but still noteworthy, importance are the overall quality of the service provided and the depth of experience of delivery personnel.

These unsurprising findings are somewhat consistent with the findings of another study published by Dow Jones & Company, Inc. This latter study showed that the reputation of a firm and experience with government regulatory matters, as well as specific experience within an industry are important factors to consider when selecting a CPA firm.[2] However, caution should be exercised when generalizing these research findings to your practice and specific marketplace. Your clients may be different from those surveyed in these two studies. They may have different service needs and be less knowledgeable about the selection of public accounting firms in general.

TABLE 4-1

**Characteristics Considered Most Important in Selecting/
Evaluating a CPA Firm**

	Corporate Financial Officers (percent)	Audit Committee (percent)	Attorneys (percent)	Nonpar- ticipating AICPA (percent)
Technical compe- tence	70	77	76	73
Overall reputation of firm	60	61	43	58
Quality of work performed	50	57	73	60
Experience in our industry	47	48	39	60
Provides a full range of auditing and related services	42	39	47	43
The overall quality of service provided	42	27	51	30
The level of experi- ence assigned to the audit team	39	30	43	39
Depth of their personnel	37	48	45	43
Quality of their SEC, tax, and consult- ing services	32	21	16	21
Worldwide coverage	27	23	22	18
Their fee structure	26	21	22	26
Their commitment to ethics	26	43	47	22
Accessibility of the partner in charge of the engage- ment	22	32	29	19
Their reputation within the profes- sion	20	25	18	21
Meeting deadlines on work	20	11	31	20
Overall ease of working with them	20	23	24	23
Convenient domes- tic offices	17	11	14	13
Reputation of top partners	12	21	10	11

Source: "An Opinion Survey of the Public Accounting Profession," sponsored by Deloitte Haskins & Sells. Conducted by Reichman Research, Inc., May 1978. Reprinted with permission. Also listed in Philip Kotler and Paul N. Bloom, "Marketing Professional Services" (Englewood Cliffs, N.J.: Prentice-Hall, 1984), p. 78.

The important point to conclude is that knowledge about what clients base their adoption decisions on is necessary information to obtain. Understanding how clients make decisions is not solely an intuitive process. Marketing research is needed to determine the "why" of buyer behavior rather than to rely on supposition. Specifically, your firm needs to determine: (1) What grouped clients (type of business, for example) consider as crucial factors in both selecting and evaluating public accounting firms. These decision points should be addressed in your promotional literature, as well as incorporated into personal sales presentations. (2) You also need to determine how clients evaluate your firm's performance on these same factors. This will help you better manage their expectations as well as identify impacting deficiencies in the production of your service.

Determining When Clients Make Decisions

The demand for some accounting services is seasonal, for example, audits, tax planning, and tax preparation services. Therefore, it is necessary to identify these services and determine when clients start the evaluation process. If corporate audit committees start their screening of public accounting firms in early summer, then you need to contact these firms at this time. If a representative of your firm contacts a prospective client in late August, it will be too late even to bid on the engagement. In situations like this your firm has to adjust to prospects' planning needs. For other kinds of services, like tax planning, there may be technical reasons why clients ought to start their assessment process earlier than they traditionally do. However, it is hard to bend the whim of demand to the will of supply.

Learned behavior is difficult to change through advertising and other mass promotional methods. Personal, face-to-face communication is better suited to changing learned behavior than mass communication. In situations like this, delivery staff has to convince clients to start the evaluation process earlier than planned. Sometimes economic incentives can be useful in overcoming client inertia while also helping the firm smooth out seasonal fluctuations in demand.

The important point is that your firm needs to determine when clients make crucial purchasing decisions. The best way to determine this is through a direct questioning approach. Staff needs to ask clients these questions: When do you reconvene the audit committee? When will the selection decision be made, and who will make this decision? Generally clients will indicate time frames if they know them. Based on this information, you have to plan to meet or stimulate demand at the indicated time, or if possible redirect demand.

Meeting demand involves the process of planning which services to promote to identified clients by specified dates. A useful technique I have used with consulting clients is the creation of a planning calendar. First, select targeted services are identified, and then a promotional plan for developing these services is discussed. This is followed by a determination of what has to be done by specific dates. Prospect lists are subsequently developed, and specific employees are held responsible for contacting these prospects by the agreed on dates. Key dates are then logged on a master planning calendar. This may appear rather bureaucratic, but planning devices such as this are necessary. It is far too easy to become involved in the day-to-day complexities of running a practice and lose sight of what has to be done and by when. Managing and meeting demand is actually a forecasting problem that involves projecting demand. However, critical due dates slip by, and this can result in lost opportunities and even clients' dissatisfaction. This is even more regrettable because the problem often can be prevented.

In summary, the complexity involved in understanding the why of client behavior essentially involves obtaining information pertaining to these grouped factors:

1. Who makes crucial purchasing decisions within an organization? What are the expectations and needs of these individuals, and who influences their beliefs and actions? In marketing parlance, assess the role and impact of KDMs, users, purchasing agents, gatekeepers, and influence agents.
2. What are the assessed needs of each client, including their motives, purchasing considerations, expectations, and prior purchasing habits? When do they decide what to purchase and from whom?
3. What factors do purchasers of accounting services consider as decisive factors in both selecting an accounting firm and evaluating a firm's performance? How do clients evaluate the performance of your firm on these same factors versus that of competitors?

MARKET SEGMENTATION

As Chapter 5 discusses, the determination of what to do and how to do it involves the formulation of a marketing strategy. A well-thought-out strategy is really a matching process. It is based on an analysis of the needs of select groups of clients, matched against the needs, strengths, and constraints of the organization. Effective strategies take into account the dynamics of the marketplace a firm competes within by determining what is possible to do. Therefore, marketing strategies help organizations realize their potential by outlining how firms ought to allocate their scarce resources.

Market segmentation is an integral part of this strategic planning process. The concept of **market segmentation** is one of breaking up this aggregate market into homogeneous groups of clients who have similar needs and interests. For resource allocation cannot be maximized if an organization tries to be all things to all clients. Why is this true? It is because markets are made up of groups of people who have different needs, interests, and receptivities toward buying select services. Once identified, it is far easier to meet the needs of these targeted clients. These separate, more homogeneous groups of clients are called **market segments**. After identifying these separate segments, then they are compared to each other. Some initial factors to compare are each segment's potentiality for expansion and how the needs and characteristics of each compare to the firm's abilities and organizational needs. Then the selected market segments that have the most promise for the firm become **target markets** that a firm plans to develop. The development of a marketing strategy then follows the selection of target markets. As discussed earlier, a marketing strategy is a marketing mix (a product, price, place, and promotional program) designed to meet the needs of target market segments, as well as those of the firm. This is why the concept of market segmentation is really a matching process.

Some CPAs erroneously believe that only the larger firms are able to employ market segmentation as a strategy. This is not a valid generalization. I have worked with many smaller public accounting firms that have targeted market segments such as farmers, automotive and heavy equipment dealers, real estate firms, restaurants, to name but a few. Remember the market is already segmented in many cases. What you as a service supplier have to decide is which segments fit your needs, limitations, and abilities. This should be done before concluding that market segmentation holds little promise for your firm.

There are three different types of strategies a firm could use. These are outlined in Figure 4-2.[3] The first strategy is called **undifferentiated marketing**, which is based on the conclusion that a firm cannot successfully employ a segmentation strategy. In essence this is a decision not to segment the market. Rather the

FIGURE 4-2

Market Segmentation Strategies

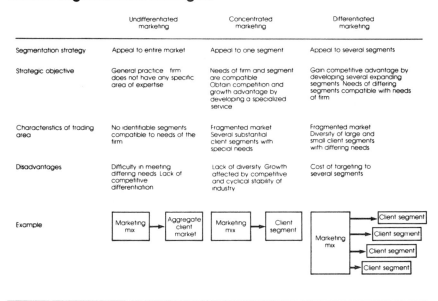

	Undifferentiated marketing	Concentrated marketing	Differentiated marketing
Segmentation strategy	Appeal to entire market	Appeal to one segment	Appeal to several segments
Strategic objective	General practice firm does not have any specific area of expertise	Needs of firm and segment are compatible Obtain competition and growth advantage by developing a specialized service	Gain competitive advantage by developing several expanding segments Needs of differing segments compatible with needs of firm
Characteristics of trading area	No identifiable segments compatible to needs of the firm	Fragmented market Several substantial client segments with special needs	Fragmented market Diversity of large and small client segments with differing needs
Disadvantages	Difficulty in meeting differing needs Lack of competitive differentiation	Lack of diversity Growth affected by competitive and cyclical stability of industry	Cost of targeting to several segments

firm decides to go after the entire market with one marketing mix, trying to attract as many clients as possible. This approach generally does not hold as much potential as the remaining two. Why is this true? It is because clients' needs are different, as is their ability to afford select services. Also, the firm may not have the ability to stimulate and service such differing needs efficiently. However, many CPA firms are afraid of limiting their practice, so they unfortunately dismiss the promise of a segmentation strategy. Also, traditional practice development lore and promotional restrictions reinforced this undifferentiated approach to practice development.

The second strategy is called **concentrated marketing** and is by far the most exclusive of the three approaches. In this approach the firm decides to go after only one target market. They then develop a marketing mix designed to fit the needs of this market. Firms that exclusively target medical practices are examples of CPA firms using a concentrated segmentation strategy. Other examples are firms that limit their practice to audits of hospitals or municipal governments. This strategy, while being the most efficient from a marketing perspective, can be a risky approach. As an industry falters, for example steel fabricating, so does the demand for accounting services for firms that service that industry. Demand for accounting services is derived demand based on the prosperity of that industry. Also, the depth and specificity of required services, and the requisite experience and technical expertise of the staff is such that many firms are not easily able to evolve into this degree of segmentation. Additionally, the issue of how much growth is attainable in a specific area, given the competitive structure of the market, can be another limiting factor. These are not meant to be perceived as absolutes supporting a reluctance even to consider a concentrated segmentation approach. Rather, they are identified as key factors to consider in your determination of what to do.

In the third approach, **differentiated marketing**, a firm decides to target several market segments by developing a unique marketing mix designed to fit the service, fee, promotion, and distribution needs of each respective segment. Price Waterhouse has identified 30 market segments calling for special marketing attention. Arthur Anderson has identified 38 industrial segments and specializes in reaching 20 of them. All "Big Eight" firms have special niches in the market. For example, Peat Marwick specifically targets insurance companies and banks, Deloitte Haskins & Sells brokerage houses, and Price Waterhouse oil and steel.[4] Smaller firms have also developed areas of specialization within their smaller trading areas.

While each marketing mix has to fit the needs of the target market, they don't always have to be totally different from one another unless specifically warranted. There will by necessity be several elements of each marketing mix similar or identical to each other. Don't be overly concerned about how clients perceive this, for clients in different segments don't generally compare and contrast specific marketing mix differences. Often the market segments will be so distinct from each other that clients within each will not interact or even read the same promotional material. Also most businesspeople are used to different approaches for different markets. For example, one element of the marketing mix, hourly fees schedules, should be different. Still some CPAs get overly concerned about charging one client a different hourly rate than another. Fee schedules have to be based on the value of the service to the client, the level of expertise involved, elasticities of demand for that service, as well as the costs involved in performing the service. After all, when you or your staff are performing different services, you are in essence selling a different product. We as consumers are used to paying different prices for different products, as well as for differing professional services. Doctors, lawyers, and consulting firms do charge different fees for the different services they render. Consequently, don't be hesitant to change an element of the marketing mix for one target market and not for another. Remember that many public accounting firms (ranging from small local firms, through the larger regional organizations, to the "Big Eight" firms) have learned the value of obtaining growth through a differentiated segmentation strategy.

One point to keep in mind when evaluating the last two strategic options is that whichever approach is selected, a firm has to incorporate that approach into its existing practice development program. For if the process of change is too abrupt, it will adversely affect client retention as well as recruitment. Additionally, client demands will continue to occupy the largest percentage of staff time. Consequently, a firm has to learn how to work smarter, and this can be accomplished by incorporating a segmentation strategy into an existing practice development program.

When identifying market segments, certain factors must be considered in an ordered fashion. Let's now turn our attention toward an understanding of these considerations.

Identifying Bases for Segmenting the Market

As Figure 4–3 indicates, there is a flow process to follow when segmenting the entire client market for public accounting services into more homogeneous segments. The first step in the process is to determine the bases for segmentation. The selected criteria should delineate the market into meaningful segments. Each segment should be heterogeneous or dissimilar to each other on the segmentation variable. Yet prospects within each segment are homogeneous, or similar to each other on the same variable. The selected criteria should also be an important, impacting distinction representing differences in demand for accounting services. For example, one frequently used basis of segmentation is segmenting the market by type of business activity, such as doctors/dentists, savings and loan banks, state banks, credit unions, diverse branches of the government (state, county, city), et cetera. However, be careful that the type of business activity does not represent meaningful distinctions in the demand for select services. For example, retailers can be large firms such as Sears, franchise outlets, department stores, car dealers, book stores, et cetera. This hypothetical grouping of retailers is not an operational market seg-

FIGURE 4-3

Market Segmentation Flow Process

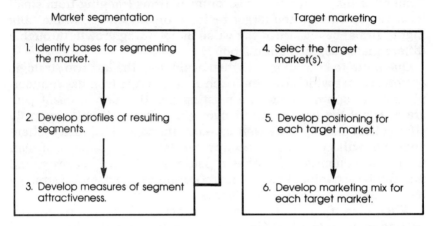

Source: Philip Kotler and Paul N. Bloom, *Marketing Professional Services* (Englewood Cliffs, N.J.: Prentice-Hall, © 1984), p. 93. Reprinted by permission of Prentice-Hall, Inc.

ment because the individuals within this grouping are not homogeneous. They all demand different services and are in different kinds of businesses.

Segmenting the market by geography and type of business is another frequently used approach. Geographic location indicates the trading area to be served, while type of business helps identify service needs. More than one basis of segmentation may therefore be necessary to delineate important distinctions representing differences in demand. For example, the segment farmers may have to be subdivided into subsegments based on acreage (size of firm). Type of business may have to be broken down into more meaningful discreet groupings, i.e. subdividing professional service suppliers into doctors/dentists, attorneys, hospitals, clinics, and the like. These are the types of decisions you will have to make when segmenting the market. Table 4-2 contains a listing of segmentation variables frequently used by public accountants for both the organizational and the consumer market.

Developing Profiles of Resulting Segments

After viable segments have been identified, then the next stage in the process is to describe each segment. This will help you in

TABLE 4-2

Segmentation Variables Used by Public Accounting Firms

Basis of Segmentation	*Examples*
Geographic	
Region	Pacific, Mountain, West North Central, West South Central, East North Central, East South Central, South Atlantic, Middle Atlantic, New England
County size	A, B, C, D
City or metro size (Population density: urban, suburban, rural)	Under 5,000; 5,000–19,999; 20,000–49,999; 50,000–99,999; 100,000–249,999; 250,000–499,999; 500,000–999,999; 1,000,000–3,999,999; 4,000,000 plus
Organizational Characteristics	
Ownership structure	Sole proprietorship, private corporations, partnerships, public corporations, governmental (city, county, state, federal)
Size of firm	Assets, revenue or sales, number of employees, et cetera
Type of business	SIC codes or business activity
Service needs (usage)	Principal accounting service required
Consumer Market	
Stage in family life cycle	Young, single; young, married, no children; young, married, youngest child under 6; young, married, youngest child 6 or over; older, married, with children; older, married, no children under 18; older, single; other
Gender	Male, female
Family size	1–2, 3–4, 5+
Household income	Income under $3,000; $3,000–$5,000; $5,000–$7,000; $7,000–$10,000; $10,000–$15,000; $15,000–$25,000; $25,000 and over
Occupational type	Professional and technical; managers, officials, and proprietors; clerical, sales; craftsmen, foremen; operatives; farmers; retired; students; housewives; unemployed
Educational attainments	Grade school or less; some high school; graduated high school; some college; graduated college

determining what clients or organizations within each segment have in common. Again the concept of homogeneity comes into play. Clients within each segment should be similar to one another in terms of their needs and service interests. This is important because it will help you in later formulating marketing mixes designed to fit the needs of each target market segment. It will also be helpful in determining your ability to service the diverse needs of market segments and in determining if these are the types of client services you wish to develop. Figure 4–4 and Figure 4–5 provide examples of two different types of segmentation matrixes. Figure 4–4 is a matrix a CPA firm used to determine which groups of clients had a need for select accounting services. Figure 4–5 is a matrix used to conceptualize differences in the market for taxation-related services.

Developing Measures of Segments' Attractiveness

Another factor in the process of identifying market segments is that once a firm has determined several likely market segments, then a decision has to be made concerning which segments to develop. The underlying rationale for this is that a firm ought to select only those segments with the most potential for development. Therefore, market segments must be screened against the following criteria:

1. The ability of the firm to service the needs of the selected segments.
2. The long-range service needs of the firm and its present position within the marketplace.
3. The competitive climate of the marketplace for those targeted services and client segments.
4. The size of the market segments a firm wishes to appeal to.
5. The projected responsiveness of clients within each segment to the promoted services, including their ability to afford the service.
6. The ability of the firm to reach the decision makers and users within the targeted segments.

If many segments meet the above criteria, then the firm has to decide which specific segments should be targeted for expansion.

Selecting the Target Markets

The issue that many firms face is how many market segments should be targeted? There is no definitive answer to this question,

FIGURE 4-4

Probable Growth Areas

Clients	Audit Securities Exchange Commission	Audit Non-Securities Exchange Commission	Financial Statement	Financial Statement	System Design	Service Bureau	Bookkeeping Assistant	Tax Preparation	Tax Planning	Other Returns	Tax Case	Cost Studies	Buy-Sell	Buy-Lease	Management Assistant
Small- to Medium-Size Businesses:															
Farmers					X				X				X	X	
Manufacturers	X				X				X				X		
Wholesalers				X	X				X			X	X	X	
Retailers		X	X						X	X			X	X	
Service organizations		X	X						X			X	X	X	
Professional:															
Medical		X	X		X				X			X			
Legal (self)			X	X					X			X			
Legal (client)															

Services

FIGURE 4–4 (concluded)

Clients	Audit Securities Exchange Commission	Audit Non-Securities Exchange Commission	Financial Statement	Financial Statement	System Design	Service Bureau	Bookkeeping Assistant	Tax Preparation	Tax Planning	Other Returns	Tax Case	Cost Studies	Buy-Sell	Buy-Lease	Management Assistant
Small- to Medium-Size Businesses (cont.):															
Professional (cont.):															
Brokerage services		X	X	X	X			X	X				X	X	
Personal service			X	X	X				X				X		
Construction					X				X			X	X		
Large businesses					X				X			X	X	X	
Nonprofit organizations												X			
Government agencies												X			X
Educational:															
Private		X							X						
Public												X			X
Proprietary		X							X						

FIGURE 4–5

Taxation Market

Market Segments	Dollar Fee Potential per Client	Ability to Attract Clients	Potential for Cross-selling Services	Attractiveness of Segment to Firm	Number of Potential Clients
Individual Tax Preparation	Low	High	Low	Low	3,000+
Individual Tax Planning	Moderate	Depends on number of tax preparation clients	Low	Moderate	500+
Business Tax Preparation	Moderate	Moderate	High	High	300–450
Business Tax Planning	Moderate	Depends on number of tax preparation clients	High	High	100–150

because the number depends on the ability of the firm to obtain and service demand. Capital resources, the expertise of the firm, the number of employees, time restraints, and present practice development efforts are indicative of the types of factors influencing the selection of target market segments.

Developing Positioning for Each Target Market

Unfortunately, many public accounting firms have limited uniqueness in the minds of prospective clients. We all know that CPA firms are not generic in capabilities, but clients are not always aware of how one firm is different from another. Yet a firm should convey a distinct image to prospective clients that differentiates that firm from competitors. This image is referred to as **market positioning**, which in a sense is a firm's personality. While some firms are characterized by a type of generic sameness, other firms have developed unique personalities through the years. These personalities are based on people's perceptions of the quality of the service (which we know means more than just technical quality), the types of services offered, fees, and other impacting factors.

One way of conceptualizing the divergent images of your firm, as well as that of competitors, is through the use of a **positioning map**. This map indicates how different firms are perceived on specific dimensions judged to be decisive factors in selecting a public accounting firm. Figure 4–6 is a **positioning map**, which indicates that the circled market segments value different things when they select public accounting firms. In this example specific client segments base their adoption decisions on their breadth of service needs, price consciousness, and the need for personalized financial counseling. For example, small manufacturers—a price conscious, larger segment of the market—are interested in hiring firms that provide a full range of advisory-related accounting services, rather than a more narrow array of reporting services. They are price sensitive clients who desire more of a consulting than a reporting service. However, in practice, different segments of the market may base their decisions on differing dimensions than those contained on this map.

Additionally, the location of competitors on this map is indicated by letters. The closer competitors are to a circle (client segment) the better they are perceived as meeting the needs of that segment. Also, the size of the market segments are indicated by the size of the circle. Larger segments indicate larger markets.

The map indicates that competitors do not appear to be fitting the needs of any one segment very well. Therefore, a firm can

FIGURE 4-6

Positioning Map

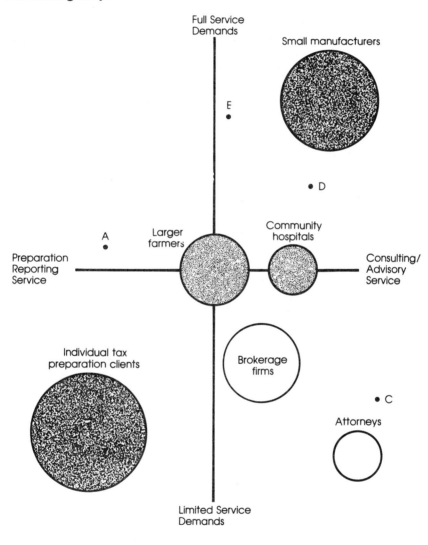

differentiate itself from competitors by developing a unique positioning targeted toward fitting the needs of specific segments. On this map farmers, community hospitals, and brokerage firms value similar attributes or dimensions when selecting a public accounting firm, although they all require different services. If a firm wishes to target any of these market segments, then it has to develop a specific mix of service offerings, fee schedules, and type of advisory service that fits the needs of these target markets.

How does one develop a positioning map such as this for a specific marketplace? A firm must conduct a cross-sectional survey of the attitudes of consumers of public accounting services within its business community. Grid dimensions on the map are determined through an involved computer mapping of the attitudes of the respondents. The number of grid dimensions, the market segments (circles), and the positions of separate firms are then plotted. The value of research-based positioning maps rests in their ability to help management conceptualize the differing needs of target markets, determine how competitors are meeting these diverse needs, and determine a firm's market position. However, managers frequently develop conceptual positioning maps based on their intuitive, more experiential, assessments of markets. Of course, the rub comes in when their assessments are not accurate.

Can a firm change its market position? Yes, it can over time if it delivers those attributes specific market segments base their purchase decisions upon. However, changing a well established market position is hard at best. After all, firms develop these reputations based on their past practices. Images emerge, and it can take quite a while to overcome preconceived notions. Fortunately, advertising what a firm stands for can greatly help in establishing a new image if the delivery system is consistent with the advertised message. For positioning of a firm is more than just developing a catchy slogan. Positioning means promoting and executing a service so that it fits the needs of the intended market segment while differentiating the firm from others.

Developing Marketing Mixes

The final stage of our segmentation process is to develop marketing mixes that address the specific needs of the target markets. As previously discussed, not every element of a marketing mix has to be unique and different for each target market. For example, service needs among target markets will no doubt be different. The nature of the service and the elasticities of demand may also require differences in fee schedules. Promotional media employed could be either different or the same depending on the circumstances. There is far less flexibility in how services are distributed than in other marketing mix elements, so on this element there is likely to be a lot of similarity. Just remember that modifications are based on unique differences in target market needs. If the differences are slight, then the needed change will be slight.

The natural tendency for public accounting firms adopting a differentiated strategy is to initially target too many segments. When too many target markets are selected, then the firm is back to the old problem of trying to be everything to too wide a cross-section of clients. Compounding this problem is the fact that when a firm targets too many client segments, they often fail to develop marketing mixes designed to fit these specific needs. For smaller firms this poses more of a threat than it does for the larger ones. Remember, the whole idea behind market segmentation is to efficiently allocate scarce resources and better service the needs of clients. This cannot be accomplished very well if scarce resources are spread too thinly across the entire market. If you have a stable, practice but would like to redirect your practice development efforts, start out modestly rather than targeting too many segments. Learn the process and the type of activity involved in successfully developing separate marketing mixes. Later you can expand the segmentation strategy as needed, after you experience the types of change and activity required. Initially targeting fewer segments gives you this needed experience and better prepares you for more ambitious efforts next year.

NOTES

1. Frederick E. Webster, Jr. and Yoram Wind, "A General Model for Understanding Organizational Buying Behavior," *Journal of Marketing*, April 1972, pp. 13–14.
2. "The Balance Sheet: Top Executives Speak Out about CPA Firms," Dow Jones & Company, Inc., 1978, p. 18.
3. These are the generally agreed on degrees of segmentation discussed in the marketing literature.
4. "Competition Comes to Accounting," *Fortune*, July 17, 1978, pp. 88–96.

PART TWO

Planning and Evaluating the Marketing Program

"For too many companies, life consists of working very hard to make small differences in performance produce small differences in profitability. But the real significant alterations in corporate fortunes depend on those relatively few and basic decisions that enable a company to fight corporate wars with its best weapons . . . not those of its competitors."

Bruce Henderson
Boston Consulting Group

The Process of Formulating a Marketing Strategy

"It has been said that there are three types of companies: Those that make things happen, those that watch things happen, and those that wondered what happened. To make things happen, your company needs strategic planning."[1]

Philip Kotler, *Harold T. Martin*
Professor of Marketing, Northwestern University

What really matters most in effectively marketing a public accounting practice? Obviously, many factors influence market success. Chapter 1 showed that maintaining a uniform degree of high quality service tops the list, although the point was established that service quality needs to be periodically assessed from clients' perspectives as well as an internal review of technical quality. Creating a responsive, market-driven organization that strives to first determine and then satisfy clients' needs is another important goal to achieve. This was the topic of discussion in Chapter 2. Chapter 3 explained that developing an effective, continuous system of acquiring marketing information is also a necessary component of success. Last, in Chapter 4 we discussed why it was so important to adopt a segmentation strategy and learn to assess clients' needs from a marketing perspective.

Yet, a firm can accomplish all of this and still fall short of realizing its goals and potentials. What is clearly lacking is the adherence to a directional strategy. In Chapter 1 we defined a **marketing strategy** as a marketing mix directed toward satisfying the needs of target markets. A marketing strategy indicates what ought to be done, whereas **tactics** concern the how of execution. An operational marketing strategy is therefore a type of directional beacon that helps steer the course of the firm. This approach is often in opposition to the more pervasive approach of appealing to the entire market with one undifferentiated marketing mix. This latter approach lacks both efficiency and specificity, which in today's environment is a far less desirable approach than a strategic perspective.

Unfortunately, the latter approach is more common because previous AICPA bans on direct solicitation, advertising, and service differentiation (implying an expertise) limited strategic alternatives for public accounting firms. Consequently, many firms have not learned to think strategically. Rather, they adhere to the status quo and fall into the trap of perpetuating traditional practice development lore.

As Figure 5–1 indicates, strategic planning is the core of strategic management and is a process-oriented method of determining what to do. Many factors can and often do exert an influence on the determination of an operational strategy. Consequently, strategic planning is not done in a type of organizational vacuum, but highly relies on an analysis of both internal and external environments.

IMPORTANCE OF A
STRATEGIC PERSPECTIVE

A strategic perspective is important for many reasons, but primarily because it is a determination of what to do, rather than a premature reliance upon how to do something, or tactics. The strategic approach collectively considers the needs of the market, the needs of the firm, competition, organizational constraints, as well as marketing opportunities. This formal, ordered process of analysis, usually results in a clearer determination of both firms' and clients' needs. Strategic alternatives generally emerge during this process of analysis. Managing partners must then decide which strategic alternative to embrace, and which to discard. After this determination, alternative tactical programs are compared in terms of poten-

FIGURE 5–1

Strategic Management Process

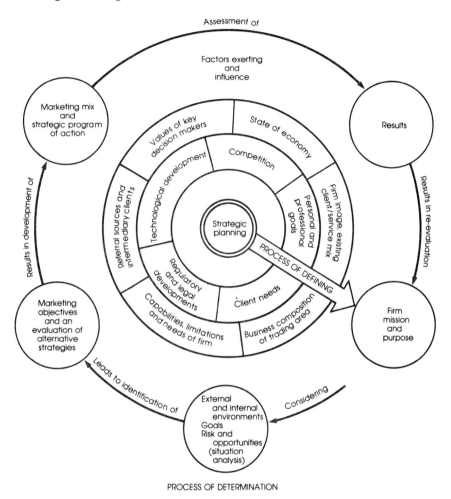

PROCESS OF DETERMINATION

Operational definitions

Goals—Personal and professional achievements (destinations).
Mission—An organization's scope, purpose, and directions.
Organizational values—A system of preferences that governs choices and trade-offs between alternate goals.

Objectives—Measurable achievements towards the attainment of a goal.
Strategy—A plan of action that promises to achieve identified objectives by developing a marketing mix targeted to specific client segments.
Program—A step-by-step plan of tactical action.

tial, cost effectiveness, and general workability. This is far better than letting fate, luck, or tradition dictate what is to be accomplished. Additionally, the concept of targeting one's efforts toward attaining specific goals and objectives is really the most efficient means of allocating organizational resources. Indeed, it is truly hard, and very inefficient from a resource perspective, to attempt to develop the entire market.

The firms that are the most effective in today's highly competitive environment are those organizations that have carefully and analytically determined what to do.[2] They have implemented a marketing strategy and are organizing their practice development efforts so they can achieve predetermined goals. In essence, they are attempting to efficiently allocate and manage their scarce personnel and cash resources. This makes far more sense than trying to achieve something that has not been specified, or spreading organizational resources so thin that little is accomplished.

A workable strategy describes what has to be accomplished and implies tactical implementation. A wise operational rule to remember is that if you, the service supplier, cannot identify how a strategy can be carried out, then the strategy is too vague to execute. This does not mean that an attainable strategy must be so explicit that a comparison of forthcoming tactical alternatives is unnecessary, for tactical alternatives, like strategies, need to be evaluated. Rather, it means that workable strategies generally imply to practicing professionals alternative tactics to consider.

At the beginning of this unit is a quote from Bruce Henderson of the highly successful Boston Consulting Group. His advice is succinct and sage. "...small differences in performance produce small differences in profitability. But really significant altercations in corporate fortunes depend on those relatively few and basic decisions that enable a company to fight corporate wars with its best weapons...not those of its competitors."[3] He was talking about carefully formulating an operational strategy, being proactive rather than merely reacting to change. In essence, he means that you should analytically determine what you wish to market to identifiable market segments and how these service offerings should be promoted, priced, and distributed. This does not mean that you have to abandon all existing clients or refuse to perform nontargeted services that your clients require. Many firms have opted to strategically market only select service offerings to targeted groups of clients, while still maintaining their existing service mixes. Growth is then more pointedly obtained through the execution of these strategies, rather than trying to inefficiently promote the entire service line.

An effective strategy, therefore, must consider a firm's present client/service mix, the nature of the practice, the firm's market position, corporate and personal goals, professional responsibilities to clients, and like factors. In essence, an effective strategy must consider which services and which client segments to maintain, which to cultivate and develop, and which to phase out. Firm and client needs, as well as market constraints, indicate the time frame in which these changes will take place.

DEVELOPING A MARKETING STRATEGY

Public accounting practices frequently evolve without a great deal of time given to a thorough audit of the practice and the marketplace. Day to day client demands and professional responsibilities do not always leave much time for analysis and reflection. Consequently, the practice evolves and changes, and it is not at all unusual to lose strategic perspective along the way.

Generally speaking, the more effective strategies are not the result of creative flashes of inspiration—a type of "Ah ha" effect one gets while taking a shower. Rather, they originate from the process of analyzing a practice. How does one develop an effective marketing strategy? One does it by following the model of analysis described in Figure 5–2, which considers specific factors in an ordered fashion. Therefore, the remainder of this chapter will discuss each stage of this ordered process.

Stage One: Situational Analysis

The first stage in the process is called a **situational analysis**, which is a type of managerial audit. In this stage you determine the needs of the client segments you wish to serve, as well as identify personal and organizational goals management wishes to attain. It is also important to identify early in this process competitive and organizational restrictions and opportunities that could either impede or enhance growth. In essence you are conducting an analysis of the present situation and clarifying goals worth attaining. At first this process may seem overwhelming, but you already know the answers to many of the questions you will be asking.

Unfortunately, what happens all too frequently is that the needed questions are never asked. That is why it is necessary to address the specific questions contained in Table 5–1. These questions were designed to help you better understand the nature of your practice and the makeup of the marketplace you compete within.

FIGURE 5-2

Development of a Marketing Strategy

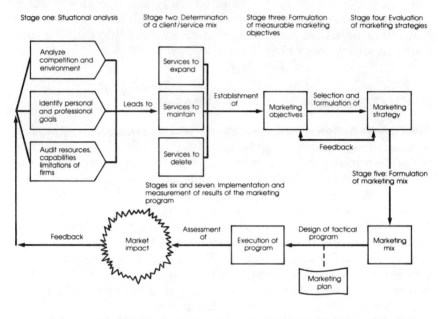

This listing is not designed to be all-inclusive, but rather a detailed indication of the types of questions you should be asking when conducting a situational analysis.

Personal and organizational goals are important to consider early in your situational analysis. However, some business authors consider a determination of goals as a second stage in the process of analysis, directly following an analysis of the market environment and the resources of the firm. Others even imply in their flow process that the development of a strategy should be linked only to corporate- or business-related goals. I support a different point of view. It is important to identify personal as well as organizational goals as early in the process of analysis as possible because what you are interested in determining is what key staff members want from the practice in terms of self-actualization, degree of specialization, growth, financial security, time commitments, and the like.

Most professionals are truly driven by this mix of personal and organizational goals. Yet, they are infrequently vocalized, less fre-

TABLE 5-1

Situational Analysis

Analysis of Your Practice

1. Determine which services bring in the most revenue.
2. Are there identifiable groups of clients who require these services (market segments)? Describe them in measurable terms.
3. Where do these clients come from? Enumerate the leading referral sources and briefly look at how you *obtained* these clients. Are potential clients within these segments accessible? If so, with what media?
4. Look to see if there is a pattern to the types of services and/or groups of clients you service. Do certain groups of clients usually require certain types of services (e.g., physicians)?
5. Are these service/client groups expandable? If so, from your existing client base, from the addition of new clients, or both?
6. Look at the services you are providing to your most important segments in terms of "benefits derived." Do the derived benefits pattern into specific categories? Are there other services that provide benefits within the same categories, which perhaps are undersold to these client segments?
7. Assess which services and/or groups of clients are decreasing in revenue-generating potential. Try to determine why and draw some conclusions. Is this evolutionary or revolutionary?
8. Do the types of services and/or groups of clients you service imply that your firm has an area of expertise that other firms do not enjoy? Could this expertise be stated as a "selling point" to potential clients?
9. Identify services you would like to expand or start offering (e.g., personal financial planning). Which groups of your present base of clients would have a need for the *benefits derived* from these services?
10. Look at the capabilities of your staff. Which areas are understaffed or overstaffed in terms of demand? Again, evolutionary or revolutionary occurrence?
11. Identify guidelines that impose growth limitations (i.e., types of services you cannot or will not offer, or number of partners the firm could support).
12. Set some tentative goals which concern:
    a. Existing services you need to continually emphasize to targeted groups of clients.
    b. New services you need to offer to identifiable groups of clients.
    c. Staffing capabilities you need to enhance or develop.
    d. Changes in prospecting or referral development efforts directed toward key clients segments.
    e. Technological or location changes (computers, branch offices, etc.).
13. How do you believe current customers rate your firm and its principal competitors, particularly with respect to reputation, service, fee schedules, and quality of services rendered?
14. Do you have measurable corporate objectives that are appropriate, given the firm's competitive position, resources, and specialization?

TABLE 5-1 *(concluded)*

Analysis of Your Practice (cont.)

15. Has your firm clearly identified the marketing tasks that must be completed before your objectives can be met? How do you periodically measure these?

Analysis of the Marketplace

16. Determine the size of your professional trading area by quickly identifying the geographic locations of your clients. Do they cluster? If so, why?
17. Is it possible to either expand your trading area (perhaps to townships or adjacent cities), or should you restrict your efforts to just the most promising section of your trading area? What is a realistic size considering the services you wish to offer, the capabilities of the firm, and the geographic concentrations of potential client groups?
18. After determining the services you wish to offer to targeted client groups, assess the substantiality of those groups within your trading area.
19. Are there other CPA firms that are aggressively seeking to develop these same types of services to similar client segments?
20. From the standpoint of a buyer of professional accounting services, try to project why a client should employ the services of your firm over another firm. Be as objective as possible.
21. What is the nature of competition among professional accounting firms in your area:
    a. Do any use targeted promotional campaigns or do the majority rely on similar "time tested" techniques of referral development, newsletters, or active involvement in a host of community organizations?
    b. Are there unwritten promotional mores you would feel uncomfortable in violating (e.g., direct mailings to *potential clients*)? Identify these.
22. How do your promotional efforts and fee structures compare to *competing* firms appealing to the same targeted groups of customers?
23. Do the differences in fee structures represent real differences in the depth, breadth, and quality of services offered by competing firms, *or* do they represent the need to cover overhead and administrative expenses? How price conscious are buyers within each segment? What are weaknesses in your major competitor's strategy?
24. Try to determine if there is a unique selling proposition for your firm that (1) enhances the image of your firm; (2) implies or states an area of professional concentration; and, (3) highlights a benefit that is important to the client. This is what should be communicated to new clients and serves as your basis for competitive differentiation.
25. How do you acquire information about changes in the marketplace? Is there any informal, yet informative, marketing information system?

quently written, but nevertheless they are present in our subconscious thoughts. If we don't achieve these unstated goals, we become dissatisfied, even though our source of dissatisfaction is not always apparent. Goals are, therefore, very important to conceptualize as early in the process of analysis as possible because, like corporate mission statements, goals help clarify and remind us of what we are really trying to accomplish.

The organizational cultures of some CPA firms, especially smaller practices, are such that personal goals have an integral role in the determination of what to do. This is less often the case in larger organizations, whether they be goods manufacturers, wholesalers/retailers, or professional service suppliers. Nevertheless, many senior staff members, and especially partners, do have the opportunity to identify what they want out of the practice they helped to create. Identifying, evaluating, and subsequently establishing shared personal and organizational goals help management to establish the corporate culture.

Stage Two: Determining a Client Service Mix

After completing a situational analysis, most firms are ready to move to the second stage of the process. In this stage management determines which services they wish to market to targeted segments of the aggregate market. Service mix decisions must specifically identify which services should be targeted for growth, maintained at some predetermined level, and deleted from the firm's offerings. These decisions will, for the most part, be based on the demand for these services by existing clients, the relative size and attractiveness of the target markets, and the firm's abilities, constraints, and opportunities. This is often a complicated decision process. Therefore, what is needed is a conceptual method of grouping service offerings so as to assess their relative worth to the organization and to determine their market demand. There are several different analytical ways of accomplishing this.

One of the first, and more popular approaches, is the **Boston Consulting Group Product Portfolio Approach.**[4] Each individual service is plotted on a matrix according to its projected growth rate and relative share of market. Market growth rate represents the annual rate of growth for that service arrayed from high to low. Market share represents a firm's percentage of the market, also arrayed from high to low. This can be measured by a ratio of a firm's billings for that service to that of a leading competitor or a more subjective, intuitive assessment can be made. What emerges

FIGURE 5–3

Boston Group Product Portfolio

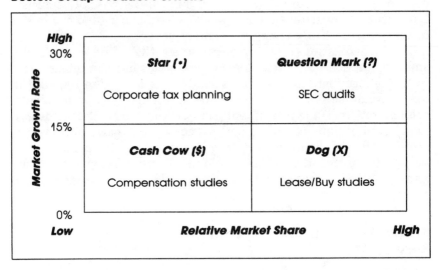

is really four different matrix positions, representing the attractiveness of that service (see Figure 5–3). Existing services are then placed in the quadrant of the matrix that best characterizes the service on the two dimensions of market share and market growth. The four different matrix positions, **stars, cash cows, question marks,** and **dogs** each call for different service mix decisions.

1. **Stars** represent those plotted service offerings for which the firm has a high share of the market in a rapid growth market. A firm will have to allocate increasing resources to stars in order just to maintain its competitive position. Maintenance is all that is often possible in a highly competitive market.

2. **Cash cows** are extremely profitable services for which the firm possesses a high market share in a low growth market. These services must be protected and maintained due to their profit potential. Cash cows also support the development of less profitable services and often allow the cross-selling of additional services. Since this is a low growth market, increasing a firm's share of market is not very easy, unless larger, direct competitors decide to withdraw from the market. Maintaining the status quo is a frequent course of action.

3. **Question marks** are so named because they represent services for which a firm has only a small share of the market in a highly competitive, growth market. Therefore, the issue is deciding whether or not it is wise to allocate organizational resources into the expansion of these service offerings versus when and how to delete select services. These are your two choices, which are greatly influenced by a determination of what leading competitors are most likely to do.

4. **Dogs** represent those services that have a low share of market in a slowly growing or declining market. Dogs contribute little to profits, they may even generate negative cash flows. However, there may be valid reasons for retaining them in the service mix. Perhaps they are necessary to offer in order to attract or retain clients, or they help reduce indirect overhead costs for other services. Most firms delete dogs from their service mix, when possible, and if not, seek a maintenance level with a slower phaseout in mind.

A limitation of the Boston Consulting Group Approach is that it does not consider organizational strengths and resources. Furthermore, this model assumes that market attractiveness can be assessed by looking at market growth rates and share of market. Yet, there are other factors to consider when evaluating the attractiveness of a market. Therefore, the BCG matrix, when used alone, may not provide the most balanced method of assessing your service mix.

General Electric, in consultation with McKinsey & Co., has devised an alternative matrix approach called **The Strategic Planning Grid**, which is described in Figure 5–4.[5] This model specifically considers two factors in arriving at service or product mix decisions: organizational strengths (the horizontal axis) and overall market attractiveness (the vertical axis).

Market attractiveness is weighted from high to low by collectively considering the size of the market, growth and profit potentials, competitive intensity, and cyclical and seasonal fluctuations in demand. The most attractive markets are therefore larger, faster growing markets, offering high profit potential, little competition, while being relatively free of cyclical and seasonal fluctuations.

Organizational strength is another high to low composite assessment that is based on a determination of existing market share, the market positioning of the firm, fee and cost structures, the quality of the firm's service offerings as compared to competitors', and knowledge of clients and service needs.

One method for determining the position of service offerings on

FIGURE 5–4

General Electric's Strategic Business Planning Grid

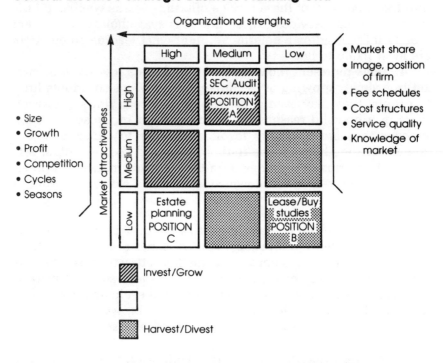

the grid is to determine the relative importance of each individual factor (weights) to the firm and the degree of attainment on that factor (values). Multiplying weights times values and then summing these products gives a composite axis score for each service. These services can then be plotted on the grid. Of course, a more intuitive assessment could also be made. However, caution is warranted because such a determination may not be supported by market data. Consequently, whenever possible, it is sound practice to have more than one person making the assessments. Differences in perspectives can then be discussed and reconciled.

The grid is divided into three zones: the three cells at the upper left hand corner (growth), the three cells at the lower right hand corner (limited growth), and, the remaining three cells running diagonally from the upper right to lower left hand corner (borderline). Let's consider the location of three hypothetical services on this grid—position A, B, and C. In position A (Security and

Exchange Commission audits for a particular industry) market attractiveness is rated as medium and organizational strength is rated as high. Therefore, a decision to expand and grow is warranted. In position B (lease/buy studies) both market attractiveness and organizational strength are low. This service offering will probably generate limited billings and may no longer warrant increased investments of time or capital. Position C (estate planning) indicates services with high market attractiveness but low on the dimension of organizational strengths. These services have to be further evaluated before determining what to do. If organizational strength cannot be improved, then a decision to delete this service offering may be prudent.

Matrixes such as these provide a very analytical, objective method of assessing the worth of select services. Either or both of these matrix approaches can be employed, but the key point to remember is that service mix decisions have to be carefully based on analysis. This analysis must consider the needs of the firm, its clients, as well as the competitive structure of the marketplace. Of course the determination of which services to promote to target markets is also based on the organizational and personal goals identified earlier in the process.

It is important to identify which services to expand, delete, and maintain because initial service mix decisions like these help identify measurable marketing objectives worth attaining. This is necessary in this stage of the process because it is impossible to determine specific marketing objectives without first determining what you wish to market and to whom. Later in the process, service offerings will again be addressed when a complete, integrated marketing mix is formulated.

Stage Three: Formulating Measurable Marketing Objectives

A **marketing objective** is a measurable goal of the business, judged by management as well as delivery staff, to be attainable at some specified future date. Marketing objectives are in part influenced by longer range organizational and personal goals. Measurable marketing objectives are important because firms develop strategies based on these objectives. Of course, marketing objectives also help determine if the strategy is working.

Therefore, they represent a deterministic indicator of what has to be accomplished as well as a diagnostic assessment of results. If you refer back to Figure 5–2 you will notice a connecting feedback arrow between formulating marketing objectives and selecting a marketing strategy. This arrow is present for a very good reason. Sometimes a firm erroneously establishes marketing objectives. Later when selecting and developing a marketing strategy, management of the firm realizes that their initial formulation of the objective was wrong. Perhaps, resources are such that management cannot realistically expect to achieve these objectives. Either the duration, level of attainment, or task itself may be in need of revision. Developing objectives and strategies is therefore a process of analysis and choice. The value of a particular course of action (objectives and strategy) becomes more apparent as time and experience progress. That is why there is a feedback loop between the two stages.

Therefore, don't be reluctant to question the probability of attaining the objective after devising the strategy. Life has taught all of us that even after careful analysis, we can be wrong in the goals we set for ourselves. Nobody has a monopoly on being right. Sometimes we just make mistakes, and the first step in solving the problem is to first admit that there is a problem.

The importance of this belief was dramatized about two years ago when I was asked to critique the marketing plan developed by a fairly large western accounting firm. The outlined strategy and tactical programs were generally well-conceived. However, the managing partner established marketing objectives, which in my view were unattainable given the resources of the firm. He admitted that they were too stringent, but he was reluctant to reevaluate his measurement criteria because he believed these objectives gave his employees "something to shoot for." Unfortunately, several of the divisional partners and their staff fell far short of attaining these unrealistic objectives. This adversely affected their performance ratings and resulted in conflict.

By the time I entered the picture, positions had solidified, and the managing partner did not want to lose face by admitting to staff that several of the objectives were unattainable. Morale was low; a few key employees did not want to continue with the marketing strategy, which was working. The whole concept of strategic planning posed a potential threat to those who witnessed this unnecessary conflict. The problem was resolved, and the managing partner, I, and delivery personnel determined more attainable objectives. However, the rigid adherence to an unobtainable goal set the entire strategic planning process in jeopardy and unnecessary conflict.

The moral to this story is twofold. First, if results are less than expected, assess both the reasonableness of the standard and the performance. Second, involve delivery staff in the development of the objectives. Their input needs to be considered when formulating operational objectives.

When creating and assessing the worth of an objective, ask yourself these questions before implementing the objectives, as well as later when assessing performance:

1. Is the objective credible and practical, or in short, worth attaining?
2. Can the objective be obtained by the specified date?
3. Has the objective been based on valid information concerning its probability of being achieved?
4. Is the objective measurable?
5. Can the objective be readily communicated to your staff, and will they be willing and able to conceptualize ways of achieving this objective?

If objectives are to serve their purpose well, they must represent a careful balance between the performance desired and the probability of their being accomplished. There are three key components all marketing objectives must possess. Marketing objectives must state the task to be accomplished, indicate the date of completion, and clearly establish a measurement criteria. When these components are present, delivery personnel and management alike are better able to agree on the objective, assess its worth, and determine its probability of being attained.

Figure 5–5 contains a listing of sample marketing objectives organized by the goal to be accomplished. They are the types of objectives a public accounting firm would set after completing a situational analysis and determining which services to target toward specific client segments. They are, therefore, both an indicator of what has to be accomplished and an assessment of results. Please notice that marketing objectives refer to more than just increasing billings. It therefore follows that marketing strategies can be designed to achieve something other than growth.

Stage Four:
Evaluating Marketing Strategies

The strategy you select should be based on the objectives you wish to accomplish. Strategies are inherently descriptive statements describing what you wish to accomplish. They can often be summarized in one or two sentences, despite the fact that considerable time may be spent in their determination. Table 5–2 describes some of the more important considerations involved in developing your

FIGURE 5-5

Model Marketing Objectives

Goal of Objective	Objective
Increase number of clients.	1. To acquire __(3)__ new clients in the __(medical services)__ area by __(1988)__ .
Increase billings in an area.	2. To increase billings by __(1989)__ in the __(estate planning)__ area by __($7,000)__ .
Diversify the mix of services.	3. To increase the __(breadth of our accounting services)__ to include the following services: estate planning, lease versus buy analysis, and computerized accounting system analysis. Targeted completion: __($6,000 annual billings)__ in each area by __(1991)__ .
Increase the number of staff.	4. To add __2__ additional CPAs to the staff by __1990__ . __(One)__ CPA must have an expertise in computerized accounting systems, and the other should be an __(MBA/CPA)__ or JD/CPA, interested in developing "management services."
Develop a specialization among existing staff.	5. To encourage our present staff to acquire some specializations in the areas of __(municipal authority)__ by __(1990)__ . (Measured by both CPE credits completed, seminars enrolled in, *and* dollar increases in this facet of the business.)

strategy. In addressing these questions, more specific goals can be formulated. For example, the marketing objective you wish to attain might concern:

1. Developing a particular line of expertise in some facet of public accounting.
2. Smoothing out seasonal demands.
3. Increasing the return on invested time through cost reduction rather than sacrificing service quality.

These are all objectives that strategic planning can help you obtain even though each will necessitate a different strategy. The first objective calls for aggressively marketing select services to targeted client segments. The second objective implies that some services should be completed, when possible, before the busy sea-

TABLE 5-2

Strategic Considerations

Target Market Segments	Service Concept	Operating Strategy	Service Delivery System
What are common characteristics of important market segments?	What are important elements of the service to be provided, stated in terms of results produced for customers?	What are important elements of strategy? Operations? Financing? Marketing? Organization? Human resources? Control?	What are important features of the service delivery system, including: The role of people? Technology? Equipment? Facilities? Layout? Procedures?
What dimensions can be used to segment the market? Demographic? Psychographic?	How are these elements supposed to be perceived by the target market segment? By the market in general? By employees? By others?	On which will the most effort be concentrated: Where will investments be made?	What capacity does it provide? Normally? At peak levels?
How important are various segments?	How is the service concept perceived?	How will quality and cost be controlled? Measures? Incentives? Rewards?	To what extent does it: Help insure quality standards?
What needs does each have?	What efforts does this suggest in terms of the manner in which the service is: Designed? Delivered? Marketed?	What results will be expected versus competition in terms of: Quality of service? Cost profile? Productivity? Morale/loyalty of servers?	Differentiate the service from competition? Provide barriers to entry by competitors?
How well are these needs being served? In what manner? By whom?			

Source: Reprinted with permission from James L. Heskett, *Managing in the Service Economy* (Boston: Harvard Business School, 1986), p. 8.

son. Other services should be pruned from the line, or not actively promoted. The third objective addresses the need to categorize your services, hire paraprofessionals for the less technically exacting services, while expanding those service offerings that can be billed at a higher fee. All of these objectives will lead to the development of different strategies and eventually the formulation of different marketing mixes.

Unfortunately, there really is no one generic listing of all possible strategies public accounting firms could pursue, although strategies can be categorized according to type. Porter in his book *Competitive Strategy: Techniques for Analyzing Industries and Competitors* offers this categorization:

1. Cost reduction.
2. Differentiation of goods or services offered by the organization.
3. Focus on a particular user group, geographic market, or portion of the product line.[6]

I believe that for public accounting firms a fourth category, stabilizing or readjusting seasonal demand for services, should be added to this listing. Regardless of how one tries to categorize services, there are some important points of similarities among the more successful strategies.

1. Business Writers Frequently Express the Belief That Better Strategies Are Based on Some Important Point of Organizational Differentiation. A. A. Thompson, Jr., and A. J. Strickland III support this belief and offer this example in their book *Strategy Formulation and Implementation:*

> Because of the strategic relevance of organizational strengths and weaknesses, it is always worthwhile for an organization to ponder what distinctive skills and capabilities it can bring to bear that will allow it to draw business away from rival organizations. Some organizations excel in manufacturing a "quality product," others in creative approaches to marketing, still others in innovation and new product development. An organization's distinctive competence is thus more than just what it can do—it is what it can do especially well as compared to rival competitors. The importance of distinctive competence to strategy rests with the unique capability it gives an organization in developing a comparative advantage in the marketplace.[7]

I believe this point of differentiation must also convey specific benefits to clients, if altering demand is the outcome you expect to achieve. Just because a strategy is based on the unique capabilities of a firm, does not mean that it is a strong enough difference to change existing patterns of demand.

Differentiation means following a different course of action from rival firms. Yet, there are specific situations where strategic imitation is an acceptable strategy to consider. The capabilities of your firm, and its present market position, may be such that you could imitate a competitor's strategy, correct any apparent weaknesses, and be more successful than the innovator. This approach is a type of innovative imitation.

In summary, look for salient points of differentiation when auditing your practice. They could be differences in an area of service specialization or expertise, cost advantages resulting in lower fees, or client benefits resulting from the way you perform the service (personalized, management-centered services of a diagnostic nature). However, don't be afraid to imitate and improve upon a successful competitive strategy, if you have the organizational capabilities to successfully do so.

2. Another Important Similarity of More Effective Strategies Rests in Their Ability to Be Easily Identified by All Those Employees Involved in the Performance of the Service. This is called a **strategic vision** and applies as well to marketing a public accounting practice as it does to marketing goods.

John Naisbitt, in his popular book *Megatrends*, offers this lucid example of a strategic vision.

> A strategic vision is a clear image of what you want to achieve, which organizes and instructs every step toward that goal. The extraordinarily successful strategic vision for NASA was "Put a man on the moon by the end of the decade." That strategic vision gave magnetic direction to the entire organization. Nobody had to be told or reminded where the organization was going. Contrast the organizing focus of putting a man on the moon by the end of the decade with "We are going to be the world leader in space exploration," which doesn't organize anything. In a constantly changing world, strategic planning is not enough; it becomes planning for its own sake. Strategic planning must be completely geared to a strategic vision and know exactly where it is going, with a clarity that remains in spite of the confusion natural to the first stages of change.[8]

What Naisbitt is saying is that the strategy must imply to all those involved in its execution an end goal that provides direction to their daily actions. For example, if a public accounting firm strategically opted to grow by responsibly increasing client billings versus expanding its client base, then they would need to develop a vision such as: To obtain growth through the staff's identification and promotion of needed accounting services to existing clients. While not as exciting as "put a man on the moon by the end of the decade," this strategic vision does provide direction to practice development efforts. This goal-oriented strategic vision specifies the behavior you expect of your staff. The expectation is that staff must identify clients' needs and become actively involved in both the promotion and the execution of a personalized service. Accent is placed on the identification, promotion, and production of accounting services that fit clients' needs. You don't have to daily tell staff what to do. They know what the vision is, but the organizational values and reward systems have to reinforce the vision. You may also have to provide training concerning how to do this. This training will no doubt vary by staff level. Otherwise, a viable vision can become a trite slogan and rightfully take its place among the many meaningless ones developed by firms who have never achieved their potentials.

3. An Effective Strategy Must Also Take into Consideration a Firm's Real Image. What does your firm represent to both present as well as prospective clients? Does your firm have some differentiating basis of expertise that contributes to its image? Are you known as problem solvers, or number crunchers? Perhaps your image is one of a traditional, highly conservative public accounting firm, not very innovative or assertive, but technically proficient. It is important to assess your image because you need to determine if there is any disparity between desired image versus actual image. If there is, then you must consider this when developing your strategy.

Images are very difficult to change by merely making adjustments in promotional programs. They cannot be easily spent into or out of existence. For example, advertising information about a firm that is contrary to clients' experiences will not alter their perceptions. In fact, those most likely to believe this advertising are prospects that know little about a firm to begin with. Advertising and other mass promotional methods are not highly effective in altering opinions contrary to observed behavior or reinforced beliefs. Prospects will merely form an initial impression, which will either be reinforced or extinguished after face-to-face interaction.

In summary, try to assess your firm's actual image, and then determine if this is the image your firm wants. If the answer is no, then you may have to change far more than your advertising and promotional programs to affect clients' perceptions. The key question to ask is, to what extent will my firm's actual image affect the performance of the market strategy?

Stage Five: Formulating a Marketing Mix

The next step is to develop a marketing mix. As previously discussed, a marketing mix is comprised of service offerings, fee schedules, promotional or communication programs, and distribution or location decisions. These are all marketing variables that can be controlled. They are called variables because they are elements that can be changed to better meet the needs of specific target markets. These variables are blended together so as to develop a cohesive program of execution that is designed to fit the needs of targeted clients, while considering the resources and limitations of the firm.

In Stage Two we discussed what to consider in making service mix decisions. The point was made that public accountants need to make decisions concerning which services to aggressively market to specific client segments. What now has to be accomplished is to review the efficacy of those earlier decisions and blend in the other crucial marketing mix variables. For, fee schedules, methods of promotion, and distribution (performance and location) have to address the needs of targeted clients, just as differing service offerings meet differing needs. This is a radical departure from conventional practice. For example, many public accounting firms establish fee levels by marking up varying staff costs by preestablished exponents. This is really a cost-plus approach to pricing and does not address specific client needs and perceptions. A manager may be billed out at $65 an hour, a partner at $95 an hour, and various levels of staff at lower rates, regardless of the service offering. However, in practice, firms often find it necessary to make fee adjustments when the client complains or the bill becomes higher than expected. Nevertheless, the cost-plus approach is not a market-oriented approach to pricing professional services. The appendix at the end of this chapter identifies the more important pricing guidelines and suggestions to consider when developing a marketing-oriented pricing strategy.

Marketing mix decisions must be tailored to the needs and characteristics of specific target market segments. This will mean different fee, promotion, and distribution mixes for different services sold to diverse client segments. This is another reason why it may be foolish to target too many groups of clients. Remember, the concept of segmentation involves tailoring marketing mixes in order to more directly service the needs of target market segments, while more efficiently allocating scarce resources. This is what you are trying to accomplish when designing a marketing mix. This may seem quite complicated at first, but remember, not every element of the marketing mix has to be changed for each target market. Some client segments will necessitate different services, which will also mean different fee schedules and promotional programs. Decisions concerning how one distributes the service will be more uniform across market segments than other marketing mix variables. Therefore, there will be unique differences, but there will also be many points of similarity among the different mixes you employ.

Stages Six and Seven: Implementation and Measuring Market Impact

These two stages are combined because in many instances soon after a strategy is implemented managers begin the process of assessing its impact. For example, consider the case of the firm that decides to promote select services to a targeted group of clients through direct mail advertising and direct response ads in trade journals. Management will start the assessment process soon after the ads have been viewed by prospects. They will no doubt base their assessment on the number of inquiries received. Therefore, for discussion purpose, these last two stages are combined, even though implementation occurs before assessment of the results.

Directly following implementation, strategies must be closely monitored and assessed against the established marketing objectives. Rarely is the tactical execution of the strategy flawless. In fact, sometimes the entire strategy has to be reevaluated because of either disappointing results or a failure to implement it as desired. Planned measurement is therefore a necessary part of the strategic process, and whenever possible multiple measures of performance should be used.

The problem of adhering to unrealistic objectives has already been discussed. The point was made that disappointing results can be attributed to an ineffective strategy, an unrealistic goal, implementation, or all of these factors. Therefore, multiple measures of performance are needed so as not to erroneously base decisions solely upon a potentially misleading factor. This can be accomplished by formulating several marketing objectives designed to measure specific facets of the strategy.

For example, suppose that a firm targets doctors and dentists and develops a marketing program designed to sell specific service offerings to clients and prospects residing in a 35 mile radius of the firm. Tactical execution of this growth strategy involves placing advertisements in medical newsletters, following up leads obtained from a direct response mail campaign, a targeted referral program, and the development of specific workshops aimed at the needs of this segment. Firm management now wishes to determine how the strategy per se is working. Also, they need to assess to what degree each tactical component of the strategy contributed to its overall success.

Determining how the overall strategy is working is the easiest of all assessment to make. Directly following implementation, management needs to compare quarterly or annual increases in billings (present clients and specific service offerings), the number of mail and telephone inquiries received, attendance at seminars, the number of new clients acquired, and like factors. Collectively, these separate measurements will help them assess overall strategic performance.

However, precisely determining the efficacy of each promotional tactic is another problem indeed. When a tactical component, such as a direct mail campaign, has been designed to generate client leads by returned coupons, cards, or telephone inquiries, then a performance assessment can be made within a few weeks. However, an assessment of how the new referral development program is working may well take over a year to determine. Sometimes the time needed to make valid assessments of specific tactics is not always compatible with annual planning needs. In these instances, performance assessments can only be made well after the strategies have been implemented.

The important point to conclude is that overall effectiveness of a strategy has to be based upon multiple measures. Determining the effectiveness of tactical components is often more difficult and may well be based on managerial intuition than on numerical measures of performance. Sometimes it is possible to assess performance soon after implementation, and in other instances a truly accurate assessment may take a year or longer to make.

NOTES

1. Philip Kotler, "Strategic Planning and the Marketing Process," *Business*, May–June 1980, pp. 2–9.
2. Peter W. Bernstein, "Competition Comes to Accounting," *Fortune*, July 17, 1976, pp. 88–96.
3. Bruce D. Henderson, *Henderson on Corporate Strategy* (Cambridge, Mass.: Abt Books, 1979).

4. See Boston Consulting Group, "The Product Portfolio," *Perspectives No. 66* (Boston: The Boston Consulting Group, 1970); George S. Day, "Diagnosing the Product Portfolio," *Journal of Marketing*, April 1977, pp. 28–38.

5. For a more detailed discussion of the GE Strategic Planning Grid refer to Charles Hofer and Dan Schendel, *Strategy Formulation* (St. Paul, Minn.: West Publishing, 1978).

6. Michael Porter, *Competitive Strategy: Techniques for Analyzing Industries and Competitors* (New York: Free Press, 1980).

7. A. A. Thompson, Jr., and A. J. Strickland III, *Strategy Formulation and Implementation* (Plano, Tex.: Business Publications, 1980).

8. John Naisbitt, *Megatrends* (New York: Warner Books, 1982), p. 94.

APPENDIX
PRICING PROFESSIONAL SERVICES

FACTORS TO CONSIDER IN FORMULATING PRICING OBJECTIVES

Pricing strategies and tactical executions of the strategy should be based on a predetermined pricing objective. Unfortunately, the majority of professional service firms make a fundamental mistake in basing their fee structures principally on cost estimates. Frequently, a measurable pricing objective has not been carefully formulated, and management merely relies on cost projections in determining fee schedules. What has been ignored or deemphasized in this "cost-plus approach" to pricing is as follows:

1. Competitive pricing and competitors' reaction to your fee approach.
2. Elasticities of demand for different service offerings (see enclosed chart).
3. Varying perceptual evaluations of fees by different client segments.
4. Maximum profit impact of alternative fee schedules.*
5. Clients' acceptance of and reaction to (growth potential) your fees.
6. The importance price plays in clients' evaluation of your firm.

*For a detailed presentation of how to calculate profit impact, please refer to Phillip Kotler and Paul N. Bloom, *Marketing Professional Services* (Englewood Cliffs, N.J.: Prentice-Hall, 1984).

Factors Clients Consider in Evaluating Price (fee charges)

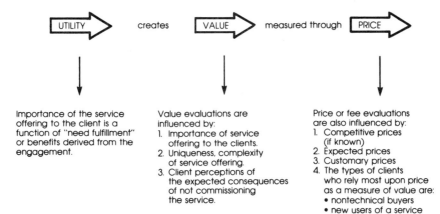

Importance of the service offering to the client is a function of "need fulfillment" or benefits derived from the engagement.	Value evaluations are influenced by: 1. Importance of service offering to the clients. 2. Uniqueness, complexity of service offering. 3. Client perceptions of the expected consequences of not commissioning the service.	Price or fee evaluations are also influenced by: 1. Competitive prices (if known) 2. Expected prices 3. Customary prices 4. The types of clients who rely most upon price as a measure of value are: • nontechnical buyers • new users of a service • consumers of specialty services

ALTERNATIVE PRICING OBJECTIVES

I. *Competitive Parity.* Price so as to *match* the price of leading competitors appealing to your targeted segments. This is a type of "don't-rock-the-boat" approach and is used when trying to:

    A. Avoid a pricing war.

    B. When nonprice competition is the way used to differentiate one firm from another.

    C. When there is a customary or expected fee range or level.

    D. When price stabilization approaches are a prudent policy to follow.

    Example: To maintain fees at a level consistent with the midpoint or average fees charged by our most direct competitors. ($50 per hour, partner level)

II. *Sales-Oriented (Market Penetration).* This is a *low* pricing approach advisable if:

    A. The market appears to be sensitive to price (elastic demand).

    B. Low fees discourage present and potential competition.

    C. Low fees are *not* viewed as an indicator of poor quality work.

    D.   Low fees attract more clients, and profit maximization is most likely possible through repeated engagements and not high markup.

Example: To set service fees below the midpoint range of fees charged by competitors appealing to the same client segments (write-up work, personal tax preparation, bookkeeping, and payroll tax preparation services).

III. *Market Skimming (Profit-Oriented).* This is a high price approach used in a profit maximization capacity when:

    A.   High fees are viewed by targeted segments as a valid indicator of service quality.

    B.   High fees *do not* attract new competitors.

    C.   Technical quality or specificity of service offering is quite specific, unique, or exacting.

    D.   Costs of meeting clients' needs do not vary appreciably as more experience and billings are acquired.

    E.   High fees do not anger clients, referral services, or third party intermediaries, such as bankers, insurance companies, brokerage firms, and so forth.

    F.   Long-range practice development is not hampered by having a select, more narrow base of high-paying clients.

Example: To charge a minimum fee of $110 per hour and to base increases of fees on uniqueness of service offering and derived client benefits. The upper fee level is established at $220 per hour.

IV. *Targeted Return.* Fee levels are set in order to reach a predetermined return on investment (time costs, capital, or both). This could result in a low, high, or parity pricing approach. This approach is frequently used by professionals who wish to earn a "fair return and provide a satisfactory" level of profits, while affording them the growth potential necessary for continued practice development.

Example: To earn 25 percent net return on 1,600 chargeable hours of time at a projected fee rate of $60 per hour (partner level).

SOME SUGGESTIONS TO CONSIDER IN PRICING PROFESSIONAL SERVICES

1.   Base your fee policies on a predetermined pricing objective. Don't ignore the cost-plus approach; rather, consider other equally important factors.

2. Develop a range of prices that reflect or consider:
   a. Elasticities of *demand* for categories of service offerings by targeted segments.
   b. Competitive fees for comparable offerings.
   c. Uniqueness, complexity, specificity of service offering as viewed by prospective clients.
   d. Growth potential and profit impact of various fee levels.
   e. Relationship between fees and intended firm image.
3. Consider quoting fees on more than just projected "per hour charges." Some considerations:
   a. Minimum fees and projected maximum fees.
   b. Retainer fee method.
   c. Stipulated dollar charge for performing a contracted service-consulting approach.
4. Evaluate how a change in your fee approach would be perceived by your *existing* clients.
5. Finally, carefully evaluate the permanence of any change in your fee approach.

SHOULD FEE SCHEDULES BE ADVERTISED?

The specific answer to this query rests in a determination of the following impacting considerations:
1. Target market considerations:
   a. Clients' knowledge of alternative, competitive fees for comparable services.
   b. Customary or expected prices for that service offering.
   c. Clients' perceived degrees of price sensitivity.
2. The uniqueness, specificity of service offering.
3. Your objective for advertising fees. What you hope to accomplish.
4. The projected effect fee advertising would have upon the image of your firm. Consider the following groups:
   a. Present clients.
   b. Prospective client segments you wish to develop.
   c. Referral sources.
   d. Competitors.
5. Prior fee levels and the frequency of upward adjustments of fees.
6. The difference between the fees charged for publicized versus unpublicized services, which require the same level of professional expertise, or which are related in some manner (i.e., tax preparation versus tax planning services).

Formulating a Practice Development Program

"A good plan, strategically executed, is better than a perfect plan next week."

George S. Patton, Jr.

A marketing strategy will remain just an idea until a firm turns it into a plan of action. Executing the idea, or strategy, can be a complicated, multidimensional task requiring the cooperation of all employees. While planning should not, but sometimes does, take place in an organizational vacuum, execution cannot. That is why practice development strategies have to be brought to life via a marketing plan. Conceptualizing the design and process of creating a marketing plan is the first topic in this chapter. Later, we discuss alternative practice development strategies.

THE ROLE AND PROMISE OF A MARKETING PLAN IN A PRACTICE DEVELOPMENT PROGRAM

Both managers and employees need to identify the types of activities they have to engage in for a marketing strategy to work.

Clearly, a plan of action is required that indicates what has to be done. This is the promise and role of a marketing plan. A **marketing plan** is the key planning document that describes:

1. A firm's strengths, weaknesses, and goals.
2. The service needs of different market segments.
3. The competitive environment of a firm's trading area.
4. An outline of the marketing strategy necessary to meet the needs of predetermined target markets.

Marketing plans are well worth the effort firms put into their development because they specifically deliver these four benefits:

1. Provide a framework for establishing goals and assessing market potential.
2. Organize promotional efforts so they achieve predetermined goals.
3. Provide continuity to a firm's growth through planning.
4. Serve as a diagnostic indicator of the type of skills, training, and competencies firms need to develop by targeted dates.

Elements of a Marketing Plan

Marketing plans are derived from an analysis of a firm's practice and the external environment. A firm is ready to draft a marketing plan after it formulates a marketing strategy. What to consider in formulating a marketing strategy was the topic of discussion in Chapter 5. Therefore, the reader may find it helpful to review Figure 5–2 for a review of this process.

There is a lot of misunderstanding among CPAs concerning what a marketing plan really is, as well as how to formulate one. Some confuse a marketing plan with an advertising or promotional schedule, or they feel it is a plan outlining public relations activities. It is neither one, although both of these promotional activities could be a part of a marketing plan.

There are many different suggested formats for marketing plans in the business literature, although some of these outlines result in relatively complicated, lengthy plans that do not address the specific needs of public accounting firms. The planning outline you select should, therefore, at minimum have these elements in common:

1. In the first section of the plan identify the factors to consider when conducting a strategic analysis of a firm's practice and trading area.

2. Follow this section with an identification of market opportunities, threats, and organizational restrictions that are
   based on this analysis.
3. Conclude the plan with a section describing short- and
   long-range goals, marketing objectives, and tactical and
   strategic programs of execution.[1]

Table 6-1 contains an abbreviated format that does meet these
prerequisites. The first section of this marketing plan is termed A
Situational Analysis of the Practice. It describes present areas of
client/service expertise, professional and personal goals of the
partners, possible client segments and the services they require,
and the competitive nature of the trading area. The firm's present
market position as well as restricting organizational limitations,
are also identified. This crucial section provides the informational foundation on which the second section of the plan will be
based.

The second section is Marketing Opportunities, Threats, and
Restrictions. In this section conclusions are drawn concerning
probable growth areas, the nature of competition and demand,
staffing limitations, and the service offerings a firm needs to
develop, expand, or delete. These conclusions allow a firm to
assess which service offerings and segments of the client market
best fit the resources of the firm.

The third section, Strategic Program Development, describes the
marketing strategy necessary to develop these client segments,
while achieving the professional and personal goals management
has specified. Specific attention is therefore given to a thorough
description of target markets and their service needs. This section
describes the marketing mix designed to meet these needs and
specific measurable marketing objectives. A description of the
types of promotional activities a firm must engage in, as well as a
projection of costs, is also contained in this section of the plan. In
fact, some firms develop an encapsulated promotional plan that
they addend to this section of the marketing plan. This encapsulated promotional plan identifies specific promotional objectives,
campaign themes, advertising media, and promotional activities a
firm has to engage in in order to execute its marketing strategy.
Often, it is this specific part of the marketing plan that is later
shared with staff who have not been involved in the formulation of
the strategy. Chapter 7 contains a sample promotional plan that has
been used for this purpose. Of course promotional plans, such as
these, are generally revised on an annual basis.

TABLE 6-1

Elements of a Marketing Plan

I. A Situational Analysis of the Practice

1. Analyze existing service offerings. Describe the nature of your services and determine what clients are really buying.
2. Identify growth restrictions (service offerings, staffing, size of trading area, etc.).
3. Compare firm's pricing, service, promotional and distribution policies with those of your closest competitors appealing to the same client mix.
4. Formulate immediate- and longer-range personal and organizational goals.
5. Describe the industrial composition of your trading area, including an analysis of the nature of competition.
6. Identify legal and ethical considerations affecting promotional mix decisions.

II. Marketing Opportunities, Threats, and Restrictions

Enumerate the conclusions you can draw from the facts discussed in the above section. These conclusions should concern:

1. Probable growth areas (client segments and services) for your firm.
2. Restrictions governing your financial, staffing, and service offerings.
3. Service offerings you have to continue to offer to specific client segments.
4. Staffing requirements, guidelines, and training program that need to be implemented or maintained.
5. Changes in marketing mix elements (services, fee schedules, promotion, and distribution).
6. Projection of the future composition of your trading area.

III. Strategic Program Development

1. Develop measurable marketing objectives. Describe how the selected strategy will help the firm achieve these objectives.
2. Identify the target markets (clients/services) you have selected and their service needs.
3. Describe the marketing mix targeted toward each segment.
4. Prepare timetables and budgets.
5. Consider delivery systems and changes in training programs, staffing requirements, and performance review system.
6. Develop a promotional plan.

THE PLANNING PROCESS

The following questions need to be answered before management initiates the planning process:

1. Who should be responsible for overseeing the development of the plan?

2. What involvement should staff have in this process?
3. What time frame does the plan encompass? Should the plan be for a year with annual revisions or longer?
4. How long will it take to compile the necessary information to draft the plan?

These decisions, and others like them, are the type of decisions management must make in the initial stages of the planning process. There are no absolute answers to these questions, and mistakes are bound to be made. Yet, there are some considerations that we now need to review in order to help assure that the planning process goes as smoothly as possible.

Who Should Develop the Marketing Plan?

The operational value of the marketing plan is directly related to who does the planning and the care they execute in analyzing the nature of the market and the capabilities of the firm. Market plans can be developed by a special task force, a standing committee of the firm, the managing partner, the director of marketing, consultants, or some combination of the above.[2] Yet, there does have to be someone in charge who has the specific responsibility of overseeing the process, specifying what has to be done, developing planning schedules, and assigning responsibilities. The first duty of this person is to describe the planning process to those charged with the responsibility for aiding in the development of the plan.

For smaller firms, the planners will no doubt be top management of the firm. They will draft the plan and execute it, and in some instances only a few people will actually be involved in its execution. For the larger firms there are a greater number of staff to select from, impacting organizational behavior issues to consider, decentralized technical specialities within the firm, and like considerations. In these environments the development of the plan will have to involve several individuals, probably coordinating their efforts through a committee.

Yet, there are some requirements planners should have in common. They should be willing draftees, have the requisite amount of time to spend, be knowledgeable about the market for public accounting services, and be involved in the execution of the plan. These are important criteria to consider when selecting the planners. For, one disgruntled member of the planning task force who believes that market planning is a waste of his or her time can either deliberately or indirectly sabotage the development of the plan. Planners must also be closely involved with clients and the execution of the services they wish to market. This will give them the needed degree of familiarity with service offerings, clients' needs, and operational problems in executing the service. Having specific knowledge about the market a firm competes within is actually more important than having experience in developing marketing plans per se.

If several people are involved in the planning process, there should be an individual who is responsible for coordinating their efforts and drafting the written plan. This individual should be a knowledgeable person of stature within the organization and be capable of influencing the decisions and behaviors of others. The managing partner is one apparent choice, but whether this is the best choice depends on both this individual and his or her relationship with the rest of the staff. For, the central planner has to have good people skills, be highly organized, delegate tasks responsibly, be very knowledgeable about clients' needs, and the competitive nature of the trading area. It is imperative that this person be receptive to the views of others, and not be dictatorial or coercive in style. If the managing partner has these attributes, then he or she would be the logical choice. If not, then another senior member of the firm should be selected.

Given these attributes, it can be a fatal mistake to appoint someone to this position who lacks the requisite stature within the organization to coordinate and oversee the planning process. This conclusion was again dramatized to me when I was asked to critique the marketing plan of an Indiana-based CPA firm. The plan was prepared by an individual with a public relations background who was recently hired in the capacity of marketing director. The position was a staff job with no line authority. She reported directly to the managing partner and her principal duties included overseeing the development of the firm's promotional pieces (firm brochures, the monthly newsletter, and manuals for client workshops), although some of the firm partners expected that she would eventually organize and coordinate practice development activities in a type of advisory fashion. Unfortunately, she was given no line authority and had a low stature within the firm. She was, nevertheless, viewed as being somehow responsible for coordinating marketing activities. Compounding this problem was the fact that several of the more influential partners had strong opinions concerning how the practice ought to be marketed. They pointedly communicated their beliefs to her, and she did her best to meld these different opinions into a cohesive plan.

Unfortunately, the result was an unworkable plan that was not based on an analysis of the practice, clients' needs, or the competitive nature of the marketplace. No strategic program or tactical execution was specified; rather, the plan was merely a wish list of goals and activities without indicating specific staff responsibilities and programs. The moral to this story is clear. Planning is the responsibility of management. As such, it cannot be easily delegated to a staff person lacking both line experience and authority. That is why it is so important to select the right person to oversee this task.

Setting Planning Horizons and Establishing Expectations

Most CPAs will have limited experience with marketing plans. Consequently, when asked to help in the development of such a plan, they may well have different expectations concerning both the content and process involved. However, if given structure and direction in terms of what to consider, they will quickly overcome this deficiency. Yet, if they do not have the interest, time, or knowledge, then their degree of participation will be limited. That is why it is wise to start the process by defining the content of a marketing plan, discussing the strategic considerations outlined in Chapter 5, and generally describing the type of activity that must take place. Responsibilities can then be assigned, planning schedules can be created, and expectations in general can be established.

Most marketing plans have a one-year planning horizon, although some firms develop five-year plans and annually update them. If your firm is inexperienced with developing marketing plans, then this latter planning horizon is generally too long. In this instance, it is better to start by developing one-year plans, although be sure to keep longer-range goals in mind when developing these. Once the plan has been formulated, management needs to periodically assess its performance, rather than waiting until the end of the year to assess results. While marketing plans are more accurately assessed at the end of the year, many managers find it necessary to make tactical revisions during the year as need arises. Don't be reluctant to make changes if you deem them necessary. Even highly experienced marketing managers find it necessary to change a plan that is not generating the expected results.

The Role of Marketing Consultants

Consultants can be helpful in specifying the content and format of the plan, as well as providing valuable marketing expertise. However, using marketing consultants as the sole planning agent charged with developing the plan is generally not a wise decision.

Consultants are not involved in the execution of the service, and they may have limited knowledge about client needs and competition. They also have no line authority within the firm and may lack the stature to get their ideas implemented. What they can provide is structure, direction, technical assistance, and objectivity. What is clearly needed in a consultant is someone who thinks strategically and is knowledgeable about what a marketing plan ought to address. Their objectivity and technical expertise can be a very valuable asset to draw upon.

An often overlooked but valuable source of marketing talent can be obtained by asking marketing educators at neighboring colleges to critique the plan or advise you during the planning process. They are knowledgeable about the strategic planning process and have the requisite professional background to help firms in need of objective counsel. This generally makes marketing educators a better choice than public relation firms, advertising agencies, or organizations selling a particular service. However, all consultants must take the time to learn about your business, evaluate your resources, and assess the practicality of your marketing plan. Consultants who come into organizations with instant answers and few questions can do more harm than good. They are the ones to avoid.

Staff's Involvement in the Execution of the Plan

To what extent should staff be aware of the strategic recommendations and tactical programs described in the marketing plan? This depends a lot on the nature of your practice. There may be key members of the firm who will be responsible for supervising the activities of others. They are going to need more background knowledge than other staff members who only need to be made aware of their individual responsibilities. Generally speaking, the entire staff should not be given the complete plan to review. If you do so, you run the risk of the plan leaking out to competitors and clients. In almost every plan, there are bound to be aspects of it that management does not wish to make public. Remember, not all employees uniformly need supporting documentation, the strategic rationale, or even the specific marketing objectives. What they do need to determine is what management's expectations are and tangible evidence that their efforts are evaluated as well as appreciated. Therefore, it is wise to address these specific, but varying, staff responsibilities in training sessions. After an appropriate time, managers and partners must periodically assess staff's performance of these tasks.

In summary, the general rule to follow is to tell staff members what they need to know in order for them to do their jobs. Training sessions, revised job descriptions, and performance appraisal reviews are the means to initially establish and assess whether or not employees are meeting management's expectation of performance.

STRATEGIC OPTIONS TO CONSIDER WHEN FORMULATING YOUR MARKETING PLAN

A firm has to first determine and then concentrate its efforts on the strategic option(s) that have the greatest potential for realizing the goals and marketing objectives management has set. There are a lot of strategic options to consider, but the following represent the ones that the majority of firms ought to review before determining what to do.[3]

Expanding Service Offerings to Existing Clients

This is one of the most attractive options for a firm to pursue because the high cost of acquiring clients has already been incurred. Additionally, staff has detailed knowledge about clients' needs and interests, and there are often mutually shared feelings of trust and respect. Consequently, the potential for meeting clients' needs through cross-selling needed services is great.[4] However, in many instances staff has to be trained in how to effectively do this. For some CPAs this is not their orientation. Consequently, training, performance appraisal, and reward systems have to reinforce this desired behavior. In Chapters 1 and 4 we discussed the intangible nature of accounting services and established the conclusion that clients look for tangible clues in assessing service quality. This means that service offerings have to be personalized, and a feeling of concern has to be conveyed to clients. Staff has to be trained in how to communicate and dramatize this concern, which for many public accountants is already present. Table 6–2 lists some suggestions concerning how to accomplish this, and suggestions such as these should be discussed in training programs.

Identifying and Cultivating High Potential Clients

In essence this is a kind of "cherry picking" approach in which you target select clients rather than all clients within a target market. Consequently, the first step in this process is to determine a client

TABLE 6-2

Techniques for Personalizing Services

1. Point out specific competencies of the firm that are not presently being used by the client. Relate these competencies to client needs.
2. Schedule a closing conference and discuss particular problems you believe deserve immediate attention. Explain to the client how your firm can help solve some of his or her problems.
3. Explain to a client the limitations of nonopinion reports.
4. Refer specialist who has had experience with this particular problem. Specialist can be from either inside or outside the firm.
5. Mention to client approaches others may have taken and management services they have employed in solving similar problems. (Remember the ethical problems of confidentiality.)
6. Send a follow-up letter to the "management letter" indicating a willingness to meet with the client and discuss particular areas discussed in the management letter.
7. Send the client informative material bearing on a problem or concern of the client. Again, mention how your firm can help in this particular matter.
8. Schedule a seminar or conference concerning an area that may be of interest to several clients. If necessary, have both staff and outside specialists (e.g., attorneys) help conduct the seminar.
9. Follow up your management letters and suggestions by creating a "turn around" file. Post dates you are supposed to respond to clients on your calendars. Develop the habit of following up correspondence concerning a new service offering with a phone call or, if possible, schedule a meeting.

screening criteria. After assessing likely candidates, those with the highest potential are the ones to target. Some factors to include in your screening system are growth and profit potential, perceived prospect dissatisfaction with existing public accounting firms, compatibility of service needs with the expertise of the firm, and accessibility of key decision makers. Separate files should be developed for each high potential prospect, and specific individuals should be assigned the responsibility for cultivating each prospect. How they go about this is often influenced by their contacts, entrepreneurial talent, and networking resources. Later, information pertaining to the percentage of clients acquired from the targeted list should be discussed, as well as an identification of what specific techniques appear to offer the most potential for expansion.

Segmenting Your Referral Development Program

Most public accounting firms have identified the same sources of referrals that many attempt to cultivate with a type of "shotgun

TABLE 6-3

Referral Development Process

Referral Sources	*Opportunities to Communicate*
Bankers	Social events
Lawyers	Lunches
Insurance agents	Participating in civic, social organizations
Brokers	Conferences/seminars
Other CPAs	Recreational events
Clients	Professional meetings
Financial consultants	Firm's literature
Alumni of the firm	Service engagements

Referral Activities

Select which groups of referrals you wish to develop. Again, the marketing plan will help point the way.

Assign particular individuals the responsibility of developing referrals from a targeted group or agent. (Financial consultants or lawyers are examples.)

Consider which techniques will work best for each group. (Newsletters, seminars, firm bulletins, brochures, etc.)

Thank each source of referral and take note of your best sources.

Concentrate on your best sources.

Remember one of the most productive sources of referrals comes from satisfied clients who indicate they are appreciative of your efforts. These people can be a walking advertisement for you.

---

approach." However, for the same reasons it is inefficient to develop the entire market, it is also inefficient to collectively develop all of these referral sources. Some will always be far more productive than others and should, therefore, receive more attention. Clearly, what is needed is a segmentation approach to referral development. By organizing your referral development efforts and assigning specific sources to individual staff members, you will be better able to expand billings through the use of referrals. In this approach, the most productive referral sources receive the most attention.

This necessitates a process of several steps involving a formalized tracking system. This system should eventually indicate which sources refer specific types of clients requiring select services. This will lead to the productive development of these referral agents. Of course, it is important to monitor the results of your targeted program, as well as express your appreciation to these agents. See Table 6-3 for an identification of possible referral sources and Table 6-4 for a listing of suggestions concerning how to develop these sources.

TABLE 6–4

Suggestions for Developing Referrals

1. Regularly scheduled luncheon meetings with professionals and clients.
2. Start a businesspersons' luncheon club.
3. Conduct "training seminars" for the staff of select clients.
4. Offer to address select groups/associations of professionals.
5. Sponsor, organize, participate in a special seminar.
6. Distribute valuable information that your clients or other professionals can use. Make sure your firm's name is prominently displayed.
   Newsletters.
   Firm's bulletins.
   Articles written by members of your firm.
7. Write "thank you" letters after you receive a new client from a referral.
8. Organize your referral efforts. This is one of the most profitable promotional efforts you are able to undertake and, in many instances, more productive than advertising.

This can be a very effective strategy, although it is seldomly used as the only strategy a firm adopts. Also, it does take time to develop an effective referral development network, and of course most competitors are also looking to do the same. Because competition is keen, you have to learn to work smarter rather than merely work longer.

Creating Favorable Awareness Programs

While this is listed in the literature as a strategic option, I question whether the building of firm awareness is a true strategy. Remember a marketing strategy involves the formulation of a complete marketing mix designed to fit the needs of both the target markets and the firm. Yet, an approach such as the preceding one does not appear to address pricing, distribution, or even service development from a strategic perspective. Rather, it is pointedly concerned with promotion of an image. Additionally, the realities of developing public relations and publicity campaigns are such that the message cannot often be specifically directed to a target market. Publicity and public relation techniques are generally promotion directed to the entire market.

Nevertheless, I believe it is important to create firm awareness, even though it is not a true strategic option. The logic underlying

TABLE 6-5

Some Suggestions for Creating Firm Awareness

1. Advertising in newspapers or trade journals.
2. Prospecting via newspaper articles written by your staff. For example, a series of tax articles written by you or your staff during the tax season.
3. Direct mailing of your firm's brochure or direct mailing informative material to *select* groupings of prospects.
4. Developing and sponsoring seminars in specific areas like estate planning. Promote these invitation-only seminars through direct mail advertising. If possible, hold the conference at a resort or hotel and combine "business and pleasure." You will attract more people with this approach.
5. *Active* involvement in civic and professional organizations (e.g., Chamber of Commerce).
6. Make your conference room available to philanthropic organizations and civic groups after business hours. Often professionals and executives serve as officers of these organizations.
7. Instruct your staff to clip news items concerning acquisitions, expansions, personnel changes, and so forth. This information can be included in existing clients' files and can also be a method of obtaining a "prospect list."
8. Whenever possible, volunteer yourself or key people as speakers for select groups (e.g., address a local teachers' union concerning tax deductions that could be of interest to them). Sometimes the local newspapers will cover this event and write an article.
9. Volunteer to serve as a guest on a local TV or radio "talk show." You may be interviewed concerning such topical areas as taxation, estate planning, or personal financial planning.
10. Approach all sources of referrals assertively. This is especially true with bankers. Don't be afraid to inform them that you wish to expand your base of clients and are, therefore, eager to expand specific services.

this approach is that a high degree of favorable publicity will eventually lead to an increase in clients. There is some truth to this since awareness of a firm is necessary before an adoption decision can be made by a potential client. Table 6-5 provides a listing of some frequently used methods of creating firm awareness directed toward both the aggregate market, as well as targeted segments. However, before embarking on an awareness campaign, a firm should attempt to determine what its image is and how, if at all, it is perceived as being different from key competitors. Many CPAs are surprised to find out that a firm's actual image is considerably different from their own beliefs. Once an image has been determined, then management is better able to diagnostically determine if this image should be reinforced in their promotional efforts. This may not always be possible, but when the opportunity arises, a firm should try to build upon its reputation.

A weakness of many awareness campaigns created by CPAs is that there is little service differentiation implied in their promotional messages. Additionally, the campaigns often appeal to the aggregate market and fail to establish the benefits of employing a particular firm. Rather, what is frequently promoted is the name of the organization and the types of services it offers. This form of promotion is far less effective than targeted, imagery advertising.

In summary, creating firm awareness is important, but awareness in and of itself may not be impacting enough to turn prospects into clients. Therefore, when used alone, this approach may not contribute as much to practice development as a true strategy.

Developing a Service or Client Specialization

As Chapters 4 and 5 explained, public accountants have to learn how to employ a segmentation approach. Several examples of firms adopting this approach have previously been discussed. Clients have different needs, and public accounting firms have to learn how to develop separate marketing mixes to fulfill these needs. This popular approach is an outgrowth of this reasoning. When employing this strategy, a firm develops a specialty in some service area, client segment, or particular industry. Three distinguishing benefits of this approach are the following:

1. Specialization greatly helps a firm position itself in the market and thereby differentiate itself from competitors.
2. Specialization permits a greater profit on volume because the firm develops "cutting edge" expertise and low cost procedures for handling similar types of engagements.
3. Specialization allows a firm to develop more efficient practice development programs and a marketing mix that addresses the needs and concerns of targeted clients.

Please remember that this approach is not just for larger firms, for smaller firms have developed specializations, even within their limited trading areas.

The key to developing a viable segmentation strategy rests in identifying which service offerings a firm can offer to substantial groups of clients who have a need for that service. Of course, whether or not that market is saturated with other competitors, as well as a firm's ability to responsibly service demand, also has to be considered. Often firms evolve into this strategic option and gradually add additional clients requiring this specialization, while they slowly phase out clients who do not have similar needs.

Replacing Marginal Clients

Some public accounting firms are unable to add on new staff and consequently find that a heavy work load leaves little time for practice development. It is not uncommon to find many of these same firms unable to bill out their time at higher rates because of clients' price sensitivity. This can result in the staff and partners working considerable hours without a satisfactory economic payoff. Eventually this will affect employee morale, service quality, and staff turnover.

What is therefore needed is an objective method of identifying candidates for pruning. Management responsibly needs to discontinue relationships with marginal clients and target the acquisition of less price-sensitive clients. This has to be done in such a manner that the reputation of the firm is not hurt. Clearly, a pruning system, tempered by individual client circumstances, has to be devised. Three important factors to consider when determining likely candidates for a gradual phase-out would be these:

1. Clients' abilities to afford contracted services.
2. Their respective growth potentials.
3. The amount of time they require during peak seasons.

After pruning, the staff is then better able to meet the demands of other clients, as well as spend more time cross-selling needed services.

NOTES

1. Robert W. Denney, "How to Develop and Implement a Marketing Plan for Your Firm," *The Practical Accountant*, July 1981, pp. 18–29.
2. For a further discussion of the pros and cons involved in different individual's developing the marketing plan see Edward W. Wheatley, *Marketing Professional Services* (Englewood Cliffs, N.J.: Prentice-Hall, 1983), pp. 53–58.
3. Philip Kotler and Richard A. Connor, Jr., "Marketing Professional Services," *Journal of Marketing*, January 1977, pp. 71–76.
4. For a more detailed discussion of the process involved in creating an internal practice development plan see Ruth J. Dumesic and Neil M. Ford, "Internal Practice Development: An Overlooked Strategy for Marketing Professional Services," *The Practical Accountant*, December 1982, pp. 33–49.

PART THREE

Promotional Mix Decisions

"If you wish in the world to advance,
your merits you're bound to enhance
you must stir it and stump it,
    and blow your own trumpet,
Or, trust me, you haven't a chance."

W. S. Gilbert

7

Promotional Planning

"Competition is one of the few commodities
where supply exceeds demand."

Promotion is a crucial element of the marketing mix as well as one
of the more glamorous aspects of marketing. The reality of a competitive marketplace is such that most businesses have to continually prospect for business in order to remain competitively viable.
Consequently, promotional messages are ubiquitous; we as consumers cannot escape them. They clamor for our attention. In fact,
some studies estimate that the typical American consumer is
exposed to over 500 advertising messages alone every day.

Yet, how many of these messages are perceived, remembered,
and acted on? A very small percentage to be sure. In fact, most
promotional campaigns fail to achieve the desired goals management has set. Why is this? Because of the volume of messages we
consumers are exposed to, we tune out most of these perceptual
stimuli. Also, many of these promotional messages are ill-conceived, the goals are unrealistic, and management has selected the
wrong promotional medium to communicate its message. Yet, this
latter point is something we as business people can do something
about. What is needed is a better identification of what is possible
to accomplish and which media are best suited for specific promotional tasks.

This is the primary objective of this unit. In this chapter we provide a marketing-oriented overview of the process and considerations involved in developing promotional campaigns. Specific attention is given to conceptualizing the uses and limitations of firm newsletters and brochures, since these media are frequently used. In Chapters 8 and 9 we turn our attention to advertising and personal selling.

THE PROMOTIONAL MIX

Promotional decisions have to be approached from a systems perspective that marketers call the **promotional mix**. The promotional mix is comprised of the following elements: sales promotion, advertising, publicity, and personal selling. Table 7–1 describes each of these elements in more detail. Each element of the promotional mix is uniquely suited for particular communication tasks, and selecting the element that best fits the communication problem at hand is a crucial decision.

For example, if the problem concerns communicating specific information (such as the firm's image) to a mass market, then advertising is generally the best choice. Targeted advertising media can be used and message content can be specified and delivered at the needed frequency, which is not the case with publicity. However, if the firm is seeking to create a favorable impression in its community and promotional funds are limited, then publicity is the logical choice. However, the content, placement, and exposure of the message is less controllable than it is with advertising. If the communication task necessitates interactive communication before any action can occur, then personal selling is the best choice. When a firm is trying to stimulate the billings of a particular type of service, then sales promotion and personal selling are logical choices.

The Three Goals of Promotional Programs

Some erroneously conclude that the only objective of a promotional campaign is to increase billings or sales. Hopefully, the result of most of your marketing activities is to increase billings, but this is not the communication objective of every campaign. As previously discussed in Chapter 4, not all buyers are ready to act after initial exposure to a message. Buyers evolve through distinct stages in the adoption process before they are actually willing to make a purchase decision. People don't frequently read an ad,

TABLE 7–1

Characteristics of Promotional Mix Elements

	Personal Selling	Advertising	Publicity	Sales Promotion
Definition	Interactive, personalized oral communication designed to persuade another to accept a particular point of view or to convince the buyer to take a specific course of action.	Paid form of nonpersonal, one-way, mass communication promoting either services or ideas sponsored by an identified sponsor (e.g., billboards, newspaper, magazine ads, and direct mail advertising).	Activities that create a favorable impression of the service, employees, or the firm in general. Nonpaid for form of mass communication (e.g., newspaper articles, sponsorship of scholarship).	Promotional activities other than publicity, advertising, and personal selling that are intended to stimulate buyer purchases (e.g., training seminars, demonstrations, and reduced fee incentives).
Message flexibility	Tailored to each prospect's needs.	Uniform and unvarying.	Beyond firm's control.	Uniform and unvarying.
Direct feedback	Yes.	No.	No.	No.
Control over message content	Yes.	Yes.	No.	Yes.
Cost per contact	The highest.	Generally the lowest.	None.	High to low.
Sponsor identification	Yes.	Yes.	No.	Yes.
Continuity of message placement	High to low depending on situation.	High to low, limited only by ability to afford more advertising.	Beyond firm's control.	Generally low.
General purpose	Secure commitment from a present or prospective client and qualify the needs of purchasers. To cross-sell additional services.	Stimulate desire, create awareness of a firm or its services.	Create a favorable impression and/or awareness of a firm.	Promote a particular service.

FIGURE 7-1

Difficulty to Change Attitudes Index

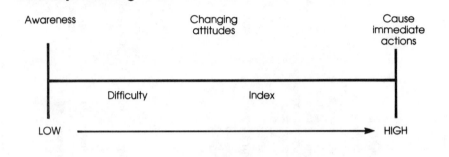

listen to a sales presentation, scan a news article, or even attend a training seminar, and then rush out and buy a product or service. Rather, potential purchasers evolve through the stages of service or firm awareness, interest, conviction, desire, and purchase. Consequently, professional service suppliers who are selling intangible services are constantly dealing with clients and prospects who are in different stages of the adoption process. It is therefore unrealistic to assume that the majority of these individuals, whether they be clients or not, are going to take immediate action after reading or hearing your message. Most will not! What is necessary is to base your communication objective on one of three possible promotional goals.

The three goals of promotion are to create awareness, to affect or change the attitudes and beliefs of others, and to cause prospects to take immediate action. Figure 7-1 describes the comparative difficulty of each of these separate promotional goals. Let's consider each of these in more detail in order to better conceptualize what is possible to accomplish. But please remember that most promotional messages should be generally based on the attainment of one of these goals. They each require different messages and assume that the prospect is in different stages of readiness to purchase.

1. To Create Awareness Is One Expected Outcome of Every Promotional Campaign. There will always be individuals who have never heard of your firm or the promoted service. For these individuals the informative nature of the promotion creates service or firm awareness. For others who are familiar with your firm or the promoted service, to remind is the expected outcome of the promotional message. Some marketers believe that reminder advertising is a separate category. Yet the purpose of reminder advertising is to provide information that may have been forgotten or encoded in prospects minds in such a manner that repeated exposure to the message is needed.

When should creating awareness be the expected outcome of a promotional campaign? When the objective of the promotion is to give prospects information they need to consider before making a decision. Later you may plan to follow up this promotion with some other activity, such as a personal visit, a client training seminar, or a direct mail campaign. For example, when a firm distributes through referral agents a brochure entitled "What to Consider in Selecting a CPA Firm," they can not realistically expect that the majority of readers will call them after scanning the brochure. The primary purpose of the brochure was to provide information, not close prospective clients. The most that can be expected from promotional pieces such as this is that the supplied information reflected favorably upon your firm and motivated some readers to act.

Remember, to create awareness is the easiest promotional goal to accomplish and a necessary one before interest, conviction, or desire can be attained. All "Big Eight" firms advertise in order to create firm awareness, which is informational advertising. Additionally, brochures, newsletters, pamphlets, bulletins, and most PR campaigns are designed to create firm and service awareness. In fact, sometimes the key objective of an informational campaign is to keep the name of the firm visible in the minds of both present and prospective clients. From a marketing prospective this objective can be important enough to warrant the continuation of this campaign.

2. Sometimes the Objective of the Promotion Is to Alter the Beliefs, Opinions, and Even Attitudes of Others. This is a far more difficult task than to merely inform or create firm awareness. Yet, it may well be the type of promotional activity that is needed. Consider the example of a firm that wishes to promote a tax planning service. Essentially they have to convince potential clients to seek professional counsel and plan for next year's taxes earlier than they have in the past. In this form of promotion, expected benefits have to be the central theme of the promotion. Just advertising the availability of the service will not cause prospects to alter previously learned behavior and take immediate action. Suitable media would be a direct-response mail campaign to existing tax preparation clients, pamphlets used as part of a sales presentation, and, to a lesser degree of effectiveness, advertisements placed in targeted periodicals.

As a general rule, the higher the degree of buyer inertia to overcome, or the more resistant to change the attitudes or behaviors are, then the less likely you are to persuade another. In fact if prospects' beliefs or opinions are generally resistant to change, then the probability of attaining your communication goal moves to the far right on the difficulty index described in Figure 7–1. If this is the situation, don't expect to change most prospects' beliefs or behavior through such mass promotion as advertising. Advertising is not a powerful enough promotional medium to overthrow conventional stereotypical beliefs. Of course, some advertisers try to spend these preconceived notions out of existence, which is often futile. Personal selling, while more expensive, is clearly the most effective method to use.

Several years ago a state CPA society asked me to critique a proposal for a $10,000 advertising campaign designed to persuade consumers that CPAs did far more than tax work. I advised them that such a campaign was a waste of money. Clearly, household consumers were not the market they needed to reach, and consumers will not quickly change long-held beliefs and stereotypical expectations based on a fleeting exposure to an advertised message. They asked me if my answer would change if they substantially increased the advertising budget. I told them that the expected outcome of changing long-held beliefs through advertising was generally an ill-conceived use of this promotional medium.

3. To Cause a Prospect to Take Immediate Action Is the Most Difficult Promotional Goal to Accomplish. This action can be commissioning a service, hiring the firm, or responding in some manner, such as requesting additional information. Human inertia is very difficult to overcome through mass promotion, and it is especially difficult through advertising. In fact, direct-response advertisers often spend in excess of 20 percent of sales on advertising. Yet, a response ratio of one half to 1 percent of list is often considered a highly successful mailing.

Frequently, public accountants express disappointment over the lack of response to their advertisements. Invariably, the vast majority of these ads were general awareness ads promoting their firms. No response was called for in the ads, and their purpose was to provide information. Therefore, in this situation trying to determine the communication effectiveness of an ad through the number of people responding is not a very accurate assessment. However, when the ad is a direct-response ad carrying a response mechanism such as a coupon or response card, then the number of people responding is a viable measurement criteria. In general, if your promotional goal is to generate a response, then the entire promotional piece has to be dedicated to this task. Therefore, be sure to make the central purpose of these ads one of generating responses.

What influences the number of people responding to a promotional piece? Several factors exert an influence, but let's review four of the more important ones:

- The relevancy of the offer or information to the prospects. Therefore, be sure to identify salient needs and provide strong reasons for taking action. An incentive, such as a cost saving, is sometimes needed to overcome prospect inertia and stimulate action.
- The composition of the audience. Are you reaching the right target market with the right message?
- The design of the promotional piece. Is it apparent that a response is requested, and have you made responding easy for prospects to accomplish?
- The promotional medium you have selected. Does it offer the requisite amount of time or space to develop your message, and does it reach the right prospects in a timely fashion?

What are the best media choices? Obviously, the ones that allow you to meet the above criteria. Often this means direct mail campaigns containing a cover letter, a response device such as a self-addressed response card, and a brochure or pamphlet. Also, using targeted journals, magazines, and specific sections of newspapers can also be appropriate media choices. Such informational media as brochures, pamphlets, and even newsletters when used alone are not as effective as these other choices. However, when used as a part of a sales presentation, they can become quite useful sales aids.

In summary, the most appealing promise of mass promotion is that it allows you to reach many more prospects at a lower per-prospect cost than personal selling. The promise of personal selling is that it is interactive, tailored to each specific situation, and a more credible form of promotion. Marketers use both in working harmony, but it is important that the possible outcomes of each promotional medium be pointedly identified before a decision is made. Remember that the higher the degree of human inertia to overcome, the lower the expected response rate. Not all services can be effectively marketed through mass promotion, rather they may have to be promoted through the more interactive medium of personal selling. One example of this is trying to promote an unsought technical service that does not immediately convey a need or benefits to potential clients.

DETERMINING PROMOTIONAL STRATEGY

Determining what to do is the first step in formulating a promotional strategy. This means that specific consideration has to be given to (1) determining the expected outcomes of your promotion, (2) formulating the theme of your message, (3) describing your target market and identifying their needs and motives, and (4) establishing the frequency and continuity of message delivery. Table 7–2 outlines these basic considerations. There are other determinants such as projected budget, the availability of affordable media, and timing constraints, which will affect your tactical decisions. However, the above four factors are really deterministic elements of your strategy. Far too frequently promotional pieces are assessed primarily from an esthetics perspective. Decisions such as the size and weight of paper and the use of color versus black and white illustrations receive more attention than determining the needs of the readers. Table 7–3 contains a brief listing of some of the common causes of ineffective promotional campaigns.

Developing Measurable Communication Objectives

A **communication objective** is a statement that indicates what is to be stated, to whom it is to be stated, and how the effect of the communication is to be measured. This degree of specificity is necessary whether the promotional material be ads, brochures, or direct mail campaigns. In most instances, several people are involved in the development and execution of a promotional piece or campaign. The sponsoring firm, printer, advertising agency, or public relation firm, all have slightly different perspectives concerning the communication task. Yet, undeniably the responsibility of determining what to say and to whom is management's responsibility. As such, it cannot be very effectively delegated to an intermediary, although intermediaries have to be made aware of the specific goals you are trying to accomplish and the target markets you are trying to reach with a specific message. Then they are

TABLE 7-2

An Identification of Four Key Marketing and Communication Factors that Affect a Promotional Campaign

1. *The outcomes you wish to attain.* These must be specified. Some examples are:

   Attract new clients.
   Provide a tax information service.
   Augment the image of the firm.
   Aid in recruiting potential employees.
   Promote under-utilized accounting services to identified client segments.

   Be exacting and analytical when formulating your goals. Most campaigns can generally accomplish only *one* task. Remember: to inform, to change the beliefs and attitudes of others, and to cause immediate action are three possible promotional goals.

2. *The content of the message:*

   Length of the message.
   Complexity or technical nature of message.
   Theme or unifying thought to be stressed.
   Referent or heart life of piece.

3. *An operational description of the target markets and their needs.* It is important to develop:

   A demographic description of the intended target market.
   A listing of the types of information relevant to this group.
   An identification of the dominant motive you need to address.
   A determination of client benefits for specific types of services.

4. *The frequency and continuity of the promotional pieces:*

   Monthly.
   Quarterly.
   Semiannually.
   Annually.
   One-time use.

---

better able to employ their expertise in selecting appropriate media and designing promotional material with the needed imagery.

The following are four components of a communication objective that have to be initially considered when formulating a promotional strategy:

1. An identification of the thought you wish to communicate or theme of your message.
2. A description of the target market.
3. A predetermined measurement criteria, including a time frame.
4. An identification of the media to be employed.

TABLE 7-3

Common Causes of Ineffective Promotional Campaigns

1. Lack of initial determination of the specific promotional goals the campaign is supposed to accomplish.
2. Failure to determine specific target markets.
3. Greater concern over graphic design and printing considerations than on developing relevant messages directed to predetermined target market segments.
4. Unnecessary budgetary and timing problems caused by initial reluctance to plan the campaign.
5. Trying to say too much or trying to accomplish too much with any one promotional piece.
6. Failure to conceptualize what types of information should and should not be included in the campaign.
7. Confusion and controversy concerning how to measure promotional campaigns. Measurement has to be based on goals that first have to be identified.

Therefore, a communication objective is a method of specifying what you wish to communicate and an identification of the expected outcomes. This will help you in determining the effectiveness of your campaign.

The following is an example of a simple, but operational communication objective used by a public accounting firm:

> To inform doctors and dentists practicing in Porter and Lake Counties that ABC Accounting Corporation specializes in providing eight (described in direct-response brochures) accounting services of direct benefit to physicians and dentists. Media employed will be a direct mail campaign comprised of a cover letter, brochure, and direct-response card. Targeted percentage of returned cards is 5 percent, and targeted increases in number of new clients acquired is set at 10 percent. The campaign will run four weeks, with one fourth of the total mailings sent each week, and will conclude December 20th.

In the preceding communication objective, the success of the promotional direct mail campaign was inferred from the number of cards returned and clients acquired. Over 700 direct mail packages were mailed. The sponsoring CPA firm felt that if it received 40 responses and was able to obtain one fourth of these prospects as clients, then the campaign would have met its objectives. Since this campaign addressed prospects' needs and requested a return response, then it was reasonable to measure its effectiveness by the number of returned cards and the number of new clients acquired. In this example the measurement criteria and expected results were in keeping with the type of promotional campaign.

Developing a Promotional Plan

Table 7–4 contains a sample promotional campaign that will help you coordinate and plan your promotional activities. It can be further modified to fit each firm's specific promotional needs. Basically, this plan starts with an enumeration of a firm's promotional objectives, a description of its target market, and an identification of its communication objectives, campaign theme, and selected media. The remainder of the plan is then devoted to a description of the tactical implementation of this strategy.

DEVELOPING EFFECTIVE NEWSLETTERS

A wide array of public accounting firms use newsletters as a practice development technique. In fact, newsletters are used by CPAs to promote their services more frequently than any other promotional medium.[1] Yet, many firms at one time or another become disgruntled over the perceived effectiveness of their newsletters. Why then have newsletters become so popular with CPA firms? These are the principal reasons:

> They are a firmly entrenched and accepted part of the acceptable practice development lore, and there are a lot of syndicated newsletters to choose from.
> They are so widely used that many firms feel awkward about not having a newsletter, so they start one.
> In the not-so-distant past, they were one of the few written promotional pieces allowed.
> They can be an effective method of informing clients as well as helping maintain firm visibility.

The most important step in the process of developing a newsletter is the initial determination of the primary task or purpose of the newsletter. After determining the primary task, then alternative communication vehicles must be compared to newsletters in terms of cost efficiency, prospect selectivity, timeliness, frequency, and continuity concerns. For example, direct mail campaigns are generally far more persuasive, selective, and action-inducing promotional media than corporate newsletters. Yet, on a per-mailing basis, newsletters are generally less expensive than most direct

TABLE 7–4

Sample Promotional Plan

Promotional objectives: (Specify goals you wish to obtain for each major part of campaign (e.g., newsletters, advertising campaign, etc.)

1. _____

2. _____

3. _____

4. _____

Target market description: (Several segments may be appealed to with different promotional vehicles and messages. Key to above objectives.)

Specific communication objectives: (Key to target market segments and promotional vehicles.)

Theme for the campaign: (If applicable, slogan or unit of meaning for each segment.)

Media mix: (Key to major parts of campaign.)
   Controlled media: (Paid-for advertising, newsletters.)

   Uncontrolled media: (Solicited publicity releases.)

TABLE 7–4 *(concluded)*

Specific promotional activities and vehicles: (Key to objectives and market segments.)

1. _____
2. _____
3. _____
4. _____
5. _____
6. _____

Describe firm's image and/or past promotional efforts: (Discuss tie-in with this campaign.)

Anticipated problems that exist or might arise: (For major parts of campaign.)

Contingency and alternative plans: (Refer to anticipated problems.)

Timetable: (List beginning and ending times for each type of promotional vehicle to be employed.)

Budget: (Anticipated costs for each part of campaign.)

Measurable responses: (Refer to goals you wish to obtain.)

Source: Adapted from Audrey Richards, ed., *Successful Public Relations Technique* (San Francisco, Calif.: Public Management Institute, 1983).

mail campaigns and can be used with more frequency, continuity, and in many instances credibility. If the firm's objective is informational, then I would opt for the newsletter. If the objective is promotional moving toward action-inducing copy, then direct mail would be my choice in most instances. It is important to make this type of comparison because newsletters are expensive, require a lot of staff time, and do convey an image, whether it be positive or negative.

Most firms find it necessary to secure the assistance of a printer in the preparation of both newsletters and brochures, although a number of CPA firms are using desk-top publishing systems to shorten the production cycle and lower costs. The appendix located at the end of this chapter contains a useful listing of guidelines to consider when working with printers and a listing of copywriting suggestions to use when promoting services. Both listings were developed for publication by the Public Management Institute.[2]

Tasks Newsletters Can Perform

Newsletters cannot close the sale and generally are not a strong enough promotional medium to cause prospects to take immediate action. Their strength lies in their informational role. However, they often have to be followed up with personal selling for action to take place. Yet, newsletters can perform several important functions:

1. Provide visibility for a firm by periodically presenting the name of the firm in a credible, informational fashion to both clients and referral sources.
2. Inform clients and/or referral sources about important changes in the legal, taxation, economic, or regulatory aspects of business.
3. Help in the promotion of underutilized accounting services by describing the need for these services within the newsletter. However, this is a secondary objective of most firm newsletters.
4. Highlight a service expertise of the firm and thereby favorably affect present and prospective clients' opinions concerning the firm.
5. Announce changes in the public accounting firm that would benefit clients. (New employees, additional services, new branch office, updated computer facilities.)
6. Inform clients and referral agents about pertinent techno-

TABLE 7-5

Personalization Techniques for Newsletters

One way to overcome a great deal of the disinterest and appeal problems of newsletters is to personalize the messages so that they are more relevant to your readers. Some techniques to consider are the following:

1. Take a general client newsletter and reposition it to those targeted market segments that you feel will really benefit from the newsletter. In your last few newsletters, announce the change and enclose a business reply card with a description of the new newsletter. Direct all interested clients to indicate on the card whether they would like to receive the new publication.

2. Have a section of the newsletter devoted to client achievement. In this section describe some noteworthy accomplishments of consenting clients (promotions, bids received, branch offices, expansion plans). An alternative to this idea is a client profile corner in which you describe the accomplishments of a client. Monthly newsletters are best suited for this latter purpose.

3. Have a section of your newsletter reserved for client promotions. Entitle it something like "Business Information Corner." Clients who are looking to exchange, barter, buy, or rent equipment can place a short announcement in the newsletter free of charge.

4. Have a section of the newsletter reserved for interesting community news concerning your principal trading area. Treat this as a "boxed section" of your newsletter and entitle it something like "What's New in ___ County" or "Business Events."

5. Periodically invite a client to write or coauthor an informative article for your newsletter. This may be a regular feature of your newsletter. One example would be to invite a prominent banker to write an article about the market and regulatory factors affecting interest rates.

6. File and index past newsletters by primary content area. Then, if a client has a particular problem or interest in a service, forward that newsletter with a brief cover letter to the client. Follow up your correspondence with a phone call.

logical, informational, or evolutionary developments in a specific field (a computer newsletter).

Newsletters can perform these tasks well. But there are many ill-conceived newsletters widely distributed by a multiplicity of firms. Consequently, a "third-class-mail image" is an obstacle to overcome. Also, the expected life of a newsletter may be quite short and its distribution within an organization limited. Generally speaking though, the severest obstacle to overcome is the lack of appeal and reader disinterest, which characterize so many newsletters. This can be partly overcome by personalizing the newsletter. Table 7-5 contains a listing of suggestions concerning how to do this.

For those firms that wish to redesign their newsletters and need to determine graphic considerations and design alternatives, I recommend the text *Publishing Newsletters* by Howard Penn Hudson.[3]

DEVELOPING EFFECTIVE FIRM BROCHURES

It is important to note that brochures are promotional/informational aids whose effectiveness is generally determined by how they are used in the communication process. Even costly, artistically constructed brochures can be ineffective as communication tools, if they contain the wrong information or are used incorrectly. The important point to remember in brochure development is to first determine who the target market is, what they need to know, and how supplying them with this information will accomplish your promotional goals. Without this initial determination, it is questionable whether a truly effective brochure will be developed. The following represents some typical uses of brochures by CPAs:

1. As a promotional/informational piece given to prospective employees.
2. As an informational piece given to clients. (Policy statements, services offered, firm mission, and so forth.)
3. As a sales presentation aid used by staff to explain the philosophy of the firm, areas of specialization, or the benefits of specific services.
4. As a promotional/referral piece left with bankers, attorneys, financial planners, et cetera. The purpose of this type of brochure is to describe the benefits of specific types of accounting services.
5. As promotional piece designed to highlight and explain certain types of services with the intent of increasing the billings in these service areas. These types of brochures are often given directly to clients.

A principal problem that CPAs encounter is trying to use a general firm brochure for too many purposes. Table 7–6 discusses this and several other pitfalls to avoid when developing brochures. One approach to use in avoiding these problems is to adhere to the ordered developmental process outlined in Table 7–7. This process will help you develop more effective brochures.

The basic point to remember is that different groups of people (clients, referral sources, prospects, and potential employees) all have different informational needs. It may appear to be cost justified to develop one general firm brochure that can be used for multiple purposes. However, this approach will often be penny

TABLE 7–6

Six Common Pitfalls to Avoid When Developing Brochures

1. The specific goals that the brochure is supposed to accomplish are not identified, but rather loosely agreed upon; general uses of the brochure seemed to be implied. Consequently, brochures are then evaluated from an aesthetic standpoint rather than from a marketing perspective.
2. Brochures are designed to accomplish several goals, and too frequently fail to accomplish any one very well. An example is that the brochure is given to new clients, prospective employees, and such referral sources as bank loan officers. All three groups are interested in different types of information and generally require different appeals.
3. Copy is far too general without any claims, specifics, or examples that readers can relate to. Sometimes propriety and complexity of material necessitates this approach, but there are numerous instances when this is not true.
4. Copy is of a CIPU classification (*clear if previously understood*). Benefits are absent, and features of the service or organization predominate. People are interested in how features translate into benefits for them.
5. Too much material is contained in the brochure, and salient pieces of information are not highlighted or ordered properly. The brochure is not too long, just not interesting to the readers.
6. The layout, use of illustrations and subheadings, and general appearance of the brochure do not invite reading or encourage message retention.

TABLE 7–7

Ordered Process to Follow When Designing Brochures

1. *Determine a theme* for the brochure that is the central thought you wish to communicate to the reader. Title of brochure and major sections should support this theme. (Theme example: "Your Professional Growth and Development with Laube and Laube, Inc.," supported by major sections of brochure stressing topical areas.)
2. *Start by listing* all the information you believe both supports your theme and is of importance to the reader and, therefore, necessary to include in the brochure. Organize this information into categories. Then assign an ordering number to the categories based on a logical sequence and the importance of the categories to the reader. This will give you a basic presentation order to follow.
3. *Subdivide the categories*, that is, firm services, into subheadings (tax, management information services, auditing, etc.). Subheadings break up the copy and facilitate reading.
4. *Select illustrations* that either directly support your theme or pointedly relate to a major section of the brochure. Illustrations can be photographs, sketches, illustrations, tables, line drawings, et cetera.

TABLE 7-7 (concluded)

5. After completing these steps, you are in a better position *to decide:* (*a*) size of the brochure: 8½" by 11", or 6" by 8", et cetera; (*b*) number of pages; (*c*) the need for and specific uses of color highlighting (color headings, color separations, color inserts, black/white, halftones, reverses, etc.); (*d*) copy styles and sizes (printers have style/size charts); and (*e*) texture, weight of paper, types of paper stock.
6. The *cover pages* are very important. Select quality heavier weight cover stock. Color is not always necessary to create a favorable first impression. Line drawings, sketches, logos, illustrations, when properly done, can be as attention-getting as color—and a lot cheaper. If possible, have the brochure theme communicated on the cover page.
7. After determining information above, obtain the appropriate size of paper and *develop a rough format* of brochure.

wise and dollar foolish, primarily because the resulting copy will not specifically address each group's informational needs. Readership will invariably suffer, and the result will be a failure to attain those promotional goals that caused you to develop the brochure in the first place.

Remember, when developing brochures, newsletters, and advertisements, you must initially determine the informational needs of the readers. Again, we find that effective marketing starts with determining the needs of those you wish to influence before engaging in any promotional activity.

NOTES

1. Philip C. Newbauer, ed., *CPA Marketing Report* (Atlanta: Robert A. Palmer, October 1982), p. 3.
2. Audrey Richards, ed., *Successful Public Relations Techniques* (San Francisco: Public Management Institute, 1983).
3. Howard Penn Hudson, *Publishing Newsletters* (New York: Charles Scribner's Sons, 1982).

APPENDIX PROMOTIONAL GUIDELINES

COPYWRITING: STYLE GUIDELINES

#	*Considerations*
1.	State the benefit to the reader in the headline and in the first copy block.
2.	Frequently use short, declarative sentences (15 words or less) and write in the present tense.
3.	Use action verbs where commitment or action is demanded.
4.	Demand an action or ask the reader to draw a conclusion. Get reader involved in your copy as early as possible.
5.	Organize your copy so the important pieces of information are listed in the first copy block:

who	when	which organization
what	how	(inverted pyramid style)
where	why	

#	
6.	Test your communication effectiveness: Is the theme or central thought of the message clear to the reader? Test this by a quick recall test of several readers.
7.	Explain or enumerate the *positive benefits* of a service to the reader.
8.	Establish your point and legitimacy with quotes, examples, or situations known to your readers.
9.	Establish your credibility. Be factual. Use *statistics* and *examples* to bolster your arguments. Avoid generalizations—especially if they can't be proven.
10.	Avoid too technical rhetoric and jargon. Use common words, which the average businessperson of reasonable intelligence would understand.
11.	Check subjects: don't switch from *I* to *he* to *they* unless it makes sense. Generally, write in the third person for brochures and newsletters. Avoid the overuse of *we* and *me*.
12.	Omit adjectives and adverbs whenever possible. "The crowd of 1,000," rather than "the extremely enthusiastic and interested crowd that was measured at 1,000."
13.	Don't let the subject and verb get too far apart. Better to break up a long sentence into two, one for each idea. This facilitates comprehension and readability.
14.	Avoid double-negatives. "They will not support an organization that will not . . . ." is too confusing; say "They will support an organization if it will . . . ."
15.	Avoid wordy complex sentences. When there is a simpler way of saying a thing, use it. Make the transitions between copy blocks logical and easy to follow.
16.	Use terms your reader can picture. Choose short, concrete words that the reader can visualize; avoid abstract terms.
17.	Tie in with your readers' experience or expectations. Relate to their situations.
18.	Write the way your clients talk. Try reading your writing aloud and changing it so that it sounds relaxed and easy to understand. Humor and warmth can be incorporated into copy to make it more interesting to the reader.
19.	Delete unnecessary words. Edit everything yourself, *two days* after you have written it.
20.	Wherever possible, use references to current topical items in the news (inflation, etc.).

Source: Reprinted with permission of Public Management Institute, 358 Brannan Street, San Francisco, CA. © 1980 Public Management Institute.

WORKING WITH THE PRINTER:
36 MONEY-SAVING TIPS

#	Item	If You Can Use
1.	Use standard sizes. Ask your printer which sizes and formats they use most often.	
2.	Use gang printing: small items that fit on one larger standard-sized paper and can be cut apart after they are printed.	
3.	Try ganging small items on the edges of larger jobs. (*Example:* Invitations, memo pads, routing slips, or business cards may fit on the waste edge of a brochure.) Keep a file of these "trim" items and use when the opportunity arises.	
4.	To print both sides of a job at one time, ask for "work and turn." Design the piece so that both front and back of the two-sided job appear side-by-side within a standard-sized or oversized printing form. For a 5,000-copy run, the first 2,500 sheets get front-and-back printing; then they are turned over to get back-and-front printing. Otherwise, all 5,000 sheets must go through the press twice, increasing your costs.	
5.	Reuse successful artwork and logos. Make photostats of the originals in different sizes; these can be pasted up on other pieces.	
6.	Don't ask for "bleed" jobs, which run to the edge of the paper. This is more expensive because the unprinted edge of the paper must be cut off after printing.	
7.	Reprint with a different color ink or paper to make an old brochure look different.	
8.	If you use color in your letterhead or news release design, or for a bulletin or newsletter, order the color run in bulk for six months or a year's paper. This saves the added cost of colored ink and registration for small daily or monthly jobs. The copy for the news releases or bulletins can be run later on the color-printed stock. (*Example:* You will mail 500 newsletters per month with two-color letterheads. You order 6,000 of different colored combinations so that you can alternate colors each month, but you will not reprint the color for a year.)	
9.	If small quantities of news release letterhead, statements, or invoices are needed for the year, have them printed with your letterhead. Add the extra words or lines on plastic overlays, or ask the printer to do this.	

(continued)

#	Item	If You Can Use
10.	Watch the weight of the paper you use. Check the actual stock you will use to be certain that it will not cost an extra stamp to mail.	
11.	Use self-mailers, when possible. You save the cost of an envelope and the time to stuff the envelopes.	
12.	Use the "toss test" to tell if your self-mailer needs an envelope or seal. If you can throw it across the room without it coming open, it can be mailed as is. Otherwise, you must seal with tape, adhesive dots, staples, or stuff in an envelope.	
13.	Check the new postal regulations to be sure that your mailers are not too small or too large for standard mailing.	
14.	Standardize your business forms. Frequently 8½ x 11 letterhead size can be used for all forms. Use different colored inks or papers to distinguish forms, if necessary.	
15.	Standardize formats and typeface used in your literature. This permits "lift and stat" use of copy and artwork from one piece to another.	
16.	Use screens to change the appearance of your text or artwork, without adding another color ink. (*Example:* Black ink with a screen looks grey or off-white, depending on how heavy the screen; brown ink looks near-black, coffee-brown, or tan.)	
17.	Use color associations for added effect: Red—strength, power, fire, passion. Yellow—energy, sun, optimism. Blue—calm, sky, clean. Green—nature, growth, fertility. Violet—Royal, religious. Rust—Maturity, harvest, stability.	
18.	Color used on one side of the print-run will show up on alternate pages in the completed, folded brochure.	
19.	Some color combinations are more effective than others at a distance: Black on yellow or orange or white. Green on white. Red on white. Navy on white or white on navy. Orange or white on black. Navy on yellow or orange.	

(continued)

#	Item	If You Can Use
20.	Avoid four-color use; it is expensive. Two or three colors are effective and less costly.	
21.	Colored envelopes are attention-getters.	
22.	Print the largest amount you could conceivably use. Setup is costly in printing; extra pieces cost a few dollars per hundred.	
23.	Avoid oversized and undersized copy. Enlargements and reductions by the printer are often limited, and they may need to enlarge something twice to get the size you want. Better to make the initial enlargements with photostats.	
24.	Plan for multi-use of pieces. Can an annual report be used as a brochure? Can a brochure be unfolded as a poster?	
25.	Avoid inserts, unless automatic inserting equipment is available for large jobs. If automatic inserting is planned, be certain that your inserts will fit the machine.	
26.	Avoid hand folding. Mechanical folders are available for most jobs; your printer may have to farm out complex or unusual folds to a bindery.	
27.	Design to eliminate waste. Use the full area of a sheet of paper. Shift to standard sizes in other paper stock if you cannot get an economical cut from the paper selected.	
28.	Be certain your paper choice will fold properly. Perfect jobs can be ruined by paper that folds imperfectly.	
29.	Combine paper orders for quantity discounts. Plan jobs ahead for six months or a year and order paper in advance.	
30.	For bulk mailing, print the bulk-mail permit directly on the mailer or envelope to avoid hand stamping each piece.	
31.	Avoid dating materials, unless it is absolutely necessary (for an upcoming event, for example, or a fund raising deadline). Subtle "dates" to be avoided: calendars in illustrations, copyright dates, trendy hair styles or clothing on models, copy references that make the mailing obsolete.	
32.	Use tissue overlays, when instructions are required. It gets confusing to mark the originals.	

(concluded)

#	Item	✓ If You Can Use
33.	Avoid close registration of colors or different elements to save time and errors in production.	
34.	Reuse artwork with: reductions and enlargements, cropping, color changes, screens, et cetera.	
35.	Avoid strip-ins, which must be added by the printer. If possible, have the pasteup artist combine all of the original material, in its correct size, on the flats.	
36.	Run postcards at the same time as envelope corners are printed. The artwork and printing setup do not change, so there is little, if any, extra change.	

Source: Reprinted with permission of Public Management Institute, 358 Brannan Street, San Francisco, CA. © 1980 Public Management Institute.

8

Advertising Public Accounting Services

"In such a go-ahead nation as the United States, it is only natural that advertising should be a very important feature of its business arrangements."

English writer **Harry Sampson** *in* A History of Advertising from the Earliest Times, 1875.

Advertising public accounting services has been a topic of debate since the controversial Bates decision in 1976. As discussed in Chapter 1, this decision substantiated professional service suppliers' right to advertise, despite code restrictions imposed by state societies. In the business literature one can find articles, position papers, and empirical studies in favor of advertising, as well as those denouncing either the "ethics" of professionals who advertise or its lack of practice development effectiveness.

Those in favor of advertising often cite the case of the San Francisco CPA firm of Siegel, Sugarman, and Seput who attribute their spectacular growth in billings from $8,000 a year to $1.75 million four years later to advertising. Also, such studies as those published in *The Wall Street Journal* reporting that surveyed attorneys on average attribute $7 in billings to every $1 in advertising expense are other strong endorsements.[1]

On the con side, the CPA firm Coleman & Grant of Newport Beach, California, cite disappointing results from their image advertising campaign, as do many other firms. Perhaps the most popular case is that of the Boston law firm Springer and Langson who went bankrupt with a $300,000 advertising campaign.[2]

Case situations such as these have contributed to the controversy concerning the value of advertising public accounting services. What then can be concluded from these opposing points of view? Basically, advertising's effectiveness relies strongly on the process a firm goes through in determining if it should advertise.

An additional source of concern for CPAs is how clients and referral sources perceive the appropriateness of CPAs advertising? Research has shown that the majority of business people are not opposed to public accountants advertising their services. In fact CPAs, as a group, exhibit the most concern over the ethics of advertising, not their clients (see Table 8–1). Therefore, the perceived professionalism of advertising is really not an area of concern for most clients. There is nothing intrinsically unethical about business people advertising a professional service to prospective clients. For advertising is neither ethical nor unethical; it is just a promotional medium such as newsletters, brochures, personal selling, and publicity. It is appropriate and suitable for specific situations; however, it is a poor choice for others. It is only the nature of what is being communicated that could make the advertised message unethical.

Nevertheless, the issue of whether or not to advertise has not been resolved to date despite arguments from either side of the controversy. What is therefore important for you as a business person to determine first· is if advertising as a practice development medium makes sense for your firm. This means that you have to be able to identify what advertising can and cannot accomplish. Secondly, you need to learn about the process and considerations involved in developing targeted advertising campaigns. The remainder of this chapter is devoted to these two topics.

ADVERTISING'S EFFECTIVENESS AS A PRACTICE DEVELOPMENT MEDIUM

Should public accountants advertise? I see no defensible, compelling reasons why they, as business people, should not use advertising when appropriate. However, this does not mean that every accountant should advertise or that advertising is a panacea for public accounting firms facing a shortage of clients. Clearly, it is

TABLE 8–1

Percentage of Respondents Agreeing or Disagreeing with Statements about CPA Advertising

Statement	Accountants			Businesspeople			t-test for Significance
	Disagree	Neither	Agree	Disagree	Neither	Agree	
1. Advertising in general is a valuable way to communicate to consumers.	18	8	74	6	5	89	yes
2. Advertising will make the public more aware of the availability of the types of services that CPAs provide.	17	14	69	5	14	81	yes
3. Advertising will improve the quality of accounting services.	81	14	5	43	43	14	yes
4. Advertising will increase competition among public accountants.	26	26	48	10	24	66	yes
5. Advertising can be tastefully used by the accounting profession.	21	17	62	11	12	77	yes
6. Advertising will lead to more specialization in the CPA profession.	30	33	37	21	33	46	no
7. Advertising by public accounting firms is inconsistent with professionalism.	31	17	52	57	20	23	yes
8. The quality of accounting services will decline as a result of advertising by the profession.	49	22	29	69	21	10	yes
9. Advertising will impair the ability of CPAs to remain independent of their clients.	51	18	31	71	17	12	yes
10. Advertising will reduce market concentration within the accounting profession.	36	53	11	40	50	10	no
11. Advertising will make the public more aware of the qualifications of specific public accounting firms.	43	18	39	20	18	62	yes

(Agree = agree or strongly agree; Neither = Neither agree nor disagree; Disagree = disagree or strongly disagree).

Source: Compiled from Scott and Rudderow, "CPA Advertising, A Research Study of Practitioner and Businessman Attitudes," *The Virginia Accountant*, June 1982.

not! Rather, the decision to or not to advertise should be based on specific marketing situations.[3] Therefore, before discussing how to advertise, let's briefly review what advertising can and cannot accomplish.

What Advertising Can and Cannot Accomplish

Advertising's greatest potential rests in its ability to inform, to create awareness, and further enhance a firm's visibility. Its promise is to deliver simple messages to large groups of targeted prospects cheaper than the more expensive medium of personal selling. Like all forms of promotion, advertising is more effective when informing than it is when trying to change attitudes or cause prospects to take immediate action.

Sometimes the success of subsequent promotional efforts depends on what clients have learned through an earlier exposure to advertising. The promise of advertising, therefore, lies in its ability to communicate a central thought to the mass market or targeted groups of clients having similar needs. Certainly it can do this far more cheaply on a cost-per-reader basis than personal selling. It can also reach prospects more frequently than personal selling, although the message is less personalized.

As Table 8–2 indicates, it is important to conceptualize what advertising can and cannot accomplish on a type of T-account perspective. Most of this is self-explanatory, but let's take a more detailed look at advertising's ability to create an image for a firm. Some erroneously conclude that advertising can create a new image for a firm. This is not generally the case because an image is a result of the fees a firm charges, the depth and breadth of service offerings, the responsiveness of the staff to clients' needs, location and age of the firm, and other factors such as these working in synergism. Images are based on both initial perceptions as well as experiences influenced by delivery systems and promotion alike. Advertising information that may be contrary to experiences will not alter clients' impressions. However, it may cause uninformed prospects to develop an initial impression of your firm, but this will change as their familiarity increases. Image advertising must be based on delivery systems clients will experience, as well as positive beliefs generally held about the firm.

Consequently, marketing research is often a necessary first step in determining these beliefs and shared experiences. These have to be translated into important (salient) benefits, and then these bene-

TABLE 8–2

What Advertising Can and Cannot Accomplish

Can Accomplish	Cannot Accomplish
1. Create awareness of a firm's services or expertise, which *could* lead to interest and prospect action.	1. Close-the-sale and/or answer prospect objections or queries. (Task of personal selling.)
2. Reach prospects at a much *lower*-cost-per-prospect than personal selling.	2. Cannot create an image for a firm.
3. Help establish or enhance an image for the firm with the artful use of graphic design and sound enhancements.	3. Cannot promote those services that are generally "unsought technical services" that do not readily convey buyer benefits.
4. Deliver a message to prospective clients of a firm difficult to reach with other promotional techniques.	4. Communicate long or complicated messages.
5. Differentiate a firm from the competition.	

fits have to be incorporated into a theme and advertised back to the market. For, nothing works quite so well in advertising as communicating information people already know to be true.

Advertising can reach thousands of people on a daily basis, but it is not very effective in communicating long or complicated messages, despite the medium employed. Rather, its potential rests in communicating conclusions that can be expressed in a sentence or two. For example, ABC firm stands for. . . , or the principal benefit of tax planning is. . . .

Advertising a professional service is different from advertising consumer goods. The intangible nature of the service necessitates that service suppliers use tangible clues in their advertising that convey service quality. A firm that advertises a long laundry list of categorized services is not using advertising very effectively. There is no central thought to perceive and no implied benefits for readers to relate to. The tangible clues concerning the intangible benefits of the service are also missing. Consequently, it is highly unlikely that any significant number of readers will even remember the name of the firm. In fact, as a group, those that have the highest probability of noticing ads such as this are other CPAs.

In summary, advertising is not the medium to use when promoting unsought technical services that do not readily convey client benefits or when communicating long, complicated messages. This is the promise of personal selling, which we discuss in Chapter 9.

Why Many Advertising Campaigns Are Ineffective

There are many ill-conceived ads and campaigns for public accounting services. What are some of the causes of these ineffective campaigns? Irwin Braun, president of a New York advertising agency, offers these seven reasons attributing to the ineffectiveness of CPA advertising:[4]

1. Failure to target the proper market segment.
2. An inability to effectively position a firm in the ad and thereby differentiate it from its competitors.
3. Running an advertisement only once or twice and not building the requisite amount of frequency.
4. Saying too much in an advertisement and not concentrating on one central idea or theme.
5. Developing bland ads, which fail to attract attention because of a poor graphic design.
6. Communicating staid facts and not service benefits.
7. Employing the wrong advertising medium that relies too strongly on newspapers.

Sometimes the expected measurement criteria (e.g., a targeted number of prospect inquiries) is not in keeping with the informational role of the ad. As we discussed earlier in Chapter 7, if the promotional objective is to generate responses, then the entire ad has to be dedicated to this task. All too frequently CPAs have unrealistic expectations concerning how to measure advertising effectiveness. The generally implied measurement criterion, short-term increases in billings, is often the wrong outcome to expect from informational advertising. Yet, it is the appropriate outcome to expect from direct-response ads promoting a specific service. Certainly, CPAs' lack of experience with advertising greatly contributes to this understandable problem.

Let's consider a firm that decides to measure the effectiveness of a purely informative image campaign via short-term increases in billings. The advertising may have effectively communicated the desired messages, but this will not always show up in immediate increases in revenue. No reader action was called for in the ads. Also, not all prospective clients who are considering changing public accounting firms are ready to act. Nevertheless, a message has been communicated that may positively affect the perceptions of prospects, referral sources, competitors, and clients alike. At the very least, this advertising (such as newsletters, brochures, or the staff's involvement in business and civic organizations) has contributed to firm visibility. In this situation, the real objective of the campaign was to communicate a specific thought, not to cause prospects to pick up the telephone and schedule an appointment. Consequently, the appropriate measurement criteria for this type of ad should be to determine how many clients, referral sources, and business prospects recall the ad and correctly perceive the message. This can be determined through advertising recall tests, if the size of the campaign and the budget allow, or through solicited feedback from clients and referral sources.

Another problem attributing to the ineffectiveness of many advertising campaigns is a failure to specifically address clients' true needs and motives. Instead, CPAs often address concerns that are important to them as professional service suppliers, rather than first determine what is important to the prospects. There can be, and often is, a considerable difference between the two perspectives.

Consider the example of a Wisconsin public accounting firm that believed that the firm's technical proficiency in accounting was the key factor clients' based their adoption decision upon. They prided themselves on the technical quality of their service and had a rather extensive internal review program to ensure this. They felt this justified their higher fees, and they continually advertised their technical proficiency with little observable effect. What went wrong? For one thing, many of the clients within their trading area believed that most public accounting firms were technically competent. Furthermore, clients did not know how to distinguish among degrees of technical acumen. What then did clients base their adoption decisions on? Marketing research showed that motives differed somewhat among market segments, but in large part the majority of clients were primarily concerned with the personalized advisory nature of the service. Of secondary consideration were fee levels and a firm's familiarity with a particular industry or line of business.

In this example, the firm was advertising something that "common sense" told them ought to be important to clients, but was not. Because of the intangible nature of accounting services, "service quality" was more closely related with the personalized advisory nature of the service than with technical proficiency. This firm should have presented in its ads tangible clues indicating its eagerness to provide a personalized service. When this firm changed its advertising to this approach, both clients' recall of the new message and the number of inquiries increased. The moral to this story is for advertising to work, you have to address salient motives. Artfully contrived, graphically appealing ads are no substitute for relevancy!

What Makes Advertising Successful

Marketing scholars know a lot more about what makes advertising ineffective than effective. Certainly avoiding the pitfalls and mistakes we have been discussing is important in the success of any advertising campaign. However, it is important to remember that advertising's effectiveness as a promotional medium is strongly related to a determination of what to say, to whom, and where the message is placed. Message theme is of crucial importance. Yet, ironically, new advertisers sometimes exhibit more concern over the graphic design of the ad and how it satisfies their personal esthetics than they do over the formulation of a message. Your focus should be to develop the message based on the needs and interests of your prospective clients. Therefore, you need to identify their motives and informational needs. Are they more or less sensitive to the price of the service in question? What do they consider important in selecting a public accounting firm? These are the kinds of questions to ask yourself before developing a campaign theme. Yet, message theme is only one of the factors that exert an influence on the effectiveness of your ads. The following considerations are also important:

1. *The selectivity of the media you have chosen to carry your message.* The media profile must match the profile of your target market. Unfortunately, many CPAs overuse newspapers, which can and often do have too broad a readership profile. The employed medium must also be able to develop the proper imagery and communicate your message at a glance. There is a lot of ad clutter in many metropolitan newspapers, and all these ads, as well as the news stories, are all vying for reader attention.

2. *The frequency of ad placement.* People recall messages not just because of the relevancy of the message but also because of their frequency of exposure to it. One-time ads are usually a waste of money. Generally, it takes several exposures to an ad before most prospects even recall the name of the advertised service or product. In most instances, a message has to have specific appeal for prospects to remember it longer than a day or two.

3. *The complexity of the message.* Far too frequently people do

not perceive the message because it is not readily understandable at a glance. Advertising, unlike news stories, is more characterized by passive rather than active readership. As such, it is not well suited for communicating long, complicated messages, but rather simple, direct conclusions. Advertising is more effective when the message is simple, direct, and communicated in a phrase or brief sentence.

4. *The market demand for the advertised service.* Advertising is better at selling services that have an established demand and convey salient benefits than it is at selling unsought technical services. That is why advertising tax preparation services generally causes more market demand than advertising an unsought technical service. Services, such as lease/buy studies, where benefits are less identifiable, are harder for prospects to relate to.

5. *The size of the market.* The client service market has to be large enough to warrant the cost of advertising. Also, the selected advertising media must be able to reach those individuals who exert a strong influence on the purchase decision.

In summary, what makes a real difference in the success of an advertising campaign is the thought you put into what to say, to whom, and in which media. The design of the ad, its ability to communicate your message, is also of key importance. Table 8–3 lists advertising guidelines to consider when formulating your message. This is not an exhaustive listing of all relevant considerations, but it does address some of the more important considerations. Adherence to these guidelines will help you to create your message effectively.

DEVELOPING AN EFFECTIVE CAMPAIGN

Figure 8–1 describes the conceptual process to follow when formulating advertising campaigns. This process pertains to the development and implementation of a campaign, rather than the creation of one or two ads. As we have previously discussed, advertising's success is strongly influenced by the frequency and continuity of message placement. One- or two-shot approaches generally yield disappointing results, unless you are promoting a seasonal service such as income tax preparation. Yet, even in a situation like this, the communication task will often necessitate several ads appearing throughout the season.

Why is it so important to follow this model process? Each stage within the process addresses specific considerations that influence

TABLE 8-3

Guidelines for Formulating an Advertised Message

In advertising, the message theme and motivational appeals are more important than an advertisement that satisfies your personal esthetics. Spend your time determining what is important to communicate to your market. If budgetary funds permit, marketing research is a necessary starting place.

1. Successful advertising first starts with an audit of your own business. This audit should determine the following:
   a. Specific *services* you wish to offer to an *identified* target market that has displayed an interest in these services or has an apparent need for these services.
   b. Translate these services into *benefits* to the *clients*. Enumerate these benefits and select only the most important or salient ones to base your communication objective upon.
2. Write out a measurable communication objective *before* you create the advertisement. This objective must state both the target market and the exact thought or message you wish to convey to this market.
3. Keep the ads simple, direct, and uncluttered. Don't try to accomplish several objectives in one advertisement. Whenever possible, make the graphics and illustrations support the copy and convey the same thought.
4. Write benefit-oriented copy and concentrate on benefits, not service features.
5. When possible, communicate the major idea in the headline. Make the headline selective, direct, and informative and address your communication theme at the beginning of the ad or commercial.
6. Make each advertisement stand on its own merits, but make the layout basically the same for each advertisement. This will give your ads a uniform look and help build name recognition.
7. Use graphics, logo, and illustrations to elicit the desired meaning and "break up" the sameness of the copy. If possible, use subcaptions below the illustrations to reinforce the message.
8. Don't expect staggering results from an ad or a few advertisements run over a short period of time. There is no such thing as an "instant success." Practice development through advertising is a planned process involving more than the placement of a few ads.

the next stage of development. For example, a market analysis has to be completed before a firm decides to advertise. If the decision to advertise is affirmative, then target markets have to be selected and their service needs assessed. Then a campaign theme can be developed. The complexity of communicating this specific message, as well as cost considerations and the demographics of the target market, will in part dictate which media to use. How often to advertise is almost always a trade-off between cost considerations and the desired degree of frequency and continuity of message

FIGURE 8-1

Marketing Management Process of Developing an Advertising Campaign

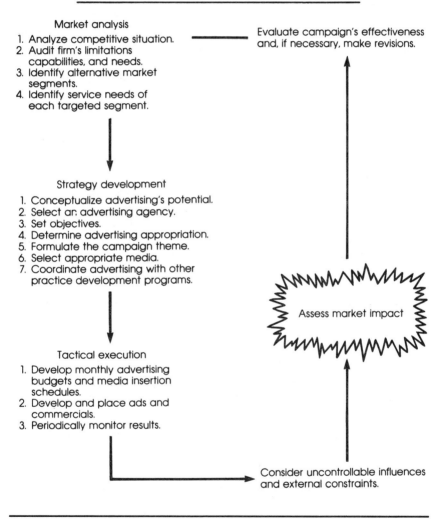

PROCESS OF DEVELOPING OF AN ADVERTISING CAMPAIGN

Market analysis
1. Analyze competitive situation.
2. Audit firm's limitations capabilities, and needs.
3. Identify alternative market segments.
4. Identify service needs of each targeted segment.

Evaluate campaign's effectiveness and, if necessary, make revisions.

Strategy development
1. Conceptualize advertising's potential.
2. Select an advertising agency.
3. Set objectives.
4. Determine advertising appropriation.
5. Formulate the campaign theme.
6. Select appropriate media.
7. Coordinate advertising with other practice development programs.

Assess market impact

Tactical execution
1. Develop monthly advertising budgets and media insertion schedules.
2. Develop and place ads and commercials.
3. Periodically monitor results.

Consider uncontrollable influences and external constraints.

placement. Get too far away from the process outlined in Figure 8–1 and the success of your campaign will suffer.

Selecting the Right Media

Generally speaking, most CPAs feel more comfortable in determining which services to promote and what to say than they do in determining which media to use. This is quite understandable because the message theme and target market are dictated by the needs of clients and the nature of the technical service. However, where to advertise and how often are less obvious choices. Selecting appropriate advertising media is really a process of comparing possible media choices on the six attributes outlined in Table 8–4. These factors often dictate which media to employ as well as which specific publications or programming to select. Let's review each consideration so that you will be better able to address appropriate issues with your advertising agencies and media representatives.

Reach refers to the number of people exposed to your message (circulation or the number of radio or TV sets tuned into that channel), whereas **selectivity** refers to the specific profile of the readers or viewers. Of key importance is reaching as many prospects within your target market as possible. For example, a metro edition of *The Wall Street Journal* may **cost** more for an ad than the same ad in the city paper. The city paper will reach more readers,

---

TABLE 8–4

Six Key Factors to Consider When Purchasing Advertising Media

1. **Reach:** The number of people *exposed* to your message.
2. **Frequency:** The number of times messages are run during a given period (month or year).
3. **Continuity:** The scheduling of the advertisements over the campaign period. For example, a steady state of five ads per month versus 50 percent of the ads the first three months and 50 percent of the ads over the last nine months.
4. **Cost:** Two factors must be considered. (1) The actual cost of the media, and (2) the comparative cost computed for cost ratios like CPM (cost per thousand).
5. **Selectivity:** The ability of the media or your campaign to reach just select prospects. The more selective the media, the higher the cost per thousand ratio.
6. **Dramatization and Persuasive Potential:** The power of the media to relay your message with sound or visual enhancements.

---

but *The Wall Street Journal* appeals more specifically to the business market. In fact, the city paper may even be cheaper on a per-column-inch basis than *The Wall Street Journal*, but the *WSJ* could still be the best media buy. As a general rule, the higher the demographic selectivity of the medium, the higher the cost in reaching a thousand readers (CPM ratio). So don't just consider the absolute or CPM cost of alternative publications without considering selectivity.

Also, some publications have a longer readership life than others. Newspapers are generally read once and then discarded over the next day or two, whereas magazines often are read several times over a much longer period of time.

Finally, remember that just because readers or viewers are exposed to the message (they subscribe to the paper or often listen to a specific station) does not ensure that they will notice your ad. True readership is only a percentage of the circulation. Therefore, each additional ad will pick up new readers as well as reinforce your message with past readers.

Frequency is the number of times the ad is run over the campaign period, whereas **continuity** refers to the pattern of exposure. Advertising often works because of both the frequency and continuity of message placement. Some research studies have shown that on average consumers have to be exposed to the same message five to seven times before they gain name recognition for the advertised firm, product, or service. This is not an absolute guideline, but rather a substantiation of the conclusion that a mix of frequency and continuity is necessary to gain even widespread name recognition. Specific patterns of ad placement will no doubt be influenced by the seasonal nature of demand, the degree of interest for the advertised service, and the general receptivity of the target market to the motivational appeal. Again, these are not absolutes, but rather specific concerns to consider.

Dramatization refers to the ability of the medium to pointedly communicate your message via sound or visual enhancements. Spot TV ads, for example, give you geographic selectivity, high frequency, and continuity of message placement, as well as provide impact by appealing to two senses. However, viewer demography is often more diverse than trade magazines, which rely exclusively on the sense of sight. Radio and outdoor ads are other media choices that provide high geographic selectivity, frequency, and continuity of message placement. However, they often lack dramatization potential because the fleeting message appeals to one sense, and, like TV, readers are not able to go back and review the message. How important is dramatization? Well, every ad or commercial must be capable of delivering the message as quickly and accurately as possible, but not all messages require a high degree of dramatization. Also, the more you are dealing with the consumer market versus the business market the more appealing TV and radio becomes.

For example, "legal clinics" that advertise low cost legal services on TV are appealing to the household consumer market. They need mass exposure, high geographic selectivity, frequency, and continuity of message placement, as well as dramatization potential. Consequently, TV provides these attributes and makes sense for these types of professional services. However, the greatest demand for public accounting services comes from the organizational and industrial markets, rather than the household consumer market. Therefore, all broadcast media in general are not as viable media choices as print media. This does not mean they cannot be effectively used in specific situations, but rather, as a generalization, they are not as well suited to the advertising of CPA services as print media.

Specific Media to Consider

Remember there are no absolutes in advertising, but there are potentialities and specific promotional needs to base your media decisions upon. Table 8–5 lists the specific attributes of these varying advertising media. Which media offer the most potential in the greatest number of situations? Direct mail, business and trade magazines, and business-oriented newspapers are the obvious choices. Let's discuss each of these in more detail.

Direct Mail.   The most selective advertising media is direct mail because it specifically allows you to reach only your present clients, or specific client segments. Also, you can personalize the message, vary the message from one market segment to another, as well as test alternative formats, direct mail lists, and appeals. There is no shortage of lists available to rent, and frequently the cost of these lists is between $50 to $100 per thousand names. You can even compile your own lists. Of importance is that a firm can elect to mail to only a portion of the list and that direct mail is a copy medium. This means that direct mail offers you more space to fully develop your message than is available in other print media. Therefore, brochures and pamphlets, accompanied by a personalized cover letter and direct response cards, are frequent elements of a direct mail campaign. Additionally, direct mail allows CPAs a greater ability to test the response-pulling potential of the list. Staff

TABLE 8-5

Media Characteristics

Newspapers	Magazines	Broadcast—TV	Broadcast—Radio	Direct Mail
1. Geographical selectivity is good	1. Good audience selectivity	1. Poor qualitative selectivity	1. Good geographical selectivity	1. High response potential
2. Prospect selectivity is poor	2. Fair geographical selectivity	2. Good geographical selectivity	2. Immediacy	2. Flexible in size, format, timing
3. Lowest cost per reader	3. Long ad life	3. Combines sight, sound, motion	3. Short life	3. Good audience selectivity
4. High-frequency potential	4. Prestige is greater than newspaper	4. Immediacy	4. Low time costs	4. Good geographical selectivity
5. Short "ad life"	5. Good reproduction, color and photo	5. Short life		5. Personal touch
6. Poorer quality in terms of color photo reproduction	6. Higher cost per issue and per reader	6. Relatively higher cost		6. High cost per person
7. Short "closing deadlines" for copy	7. Time delay in publishing	7. High impact		
	8. Longer closing deadlines for space			

can then follow up returned responses with a phone call, office visit, or another mailing. These are important attributes of direct mail, which make it quite suitable for business-to-business advertising.

Some CPAs reject direct mail as a viable medium because of their perception of the "ethics" of direct solicitation, or because of this medium's perceived image. Both business people, as well as household consumers, are increasingly receiving more direct mail advertising, which adds to the junk mail image. However, studies by the U.S. Post Office do indicate that the majority of direct mail advertising is opened, rather than thrown away unopened. Consequently, readership is not as low as many laymen think. The article "Advertising on a Limited Budget: A Small Firm's Experience" describes how one firm successfully used direct mail and newspaper advertising to achieve its promotional objectives.[5] Firms considering direct mail advertising will find this article helpful.

Business and Trade Magazines. The value of these publications rests in their ability to selectively reach specific segments of the market. Another advantage of trade publications is their life span. Frequently, business and trade magazines are kept for several months before being discarded. In this respect, they are unlike direct mail campaigns, in which the decision to keep or discard the promotional material is often made immediately after opening the envelope.

Trade and business magazines are not as geographically and demographically selective as direct mail, but they do allow firms a less labor-intensive means of reaching specific market segments. By using several publications and running repeat ads throughout the promotional period CPAs can more effectively reach a large percentage of the target market than is often possible when mailing to a rented list. Of course, many prospects could be outside of a firm's trading area. Trade publications are also often perceived as a more "upscale medium" than direct mail. As such, they are a more appropriate medium for imagery advertising. Finally, many specialized industry publications have reader response cards on which readers indicate which specific advertisement they would like to receive information about. The publication then sends to each advertiser a list of prospects that can be targeted in a direct mail campaign.

Therefore, as a media choice, trade publications offer many advantages. Yet, of crucial importance is the identification of which publications to advertise in. This can be determined by referring to *Standard Rate and Data Service (SRDS)*, a media reference source for the advertising profession. Most major metropolitan libraries and advertising agencies subscribe to SRDS, which categorizes and lists magazines, newspapers, radio, and TV stations. Advertising agencies use SRDS in conducting a media search before selecting specific publications. It is fairly easy to use and can provide useful comparative information concerning the cost, selectivity, and reach of each listed medium.

Newspapers. I have heard more dissatisfaction over the lack of results from newspaper advertising than any other medium. In the majority of these instances, the advertisements were small, infrequently placed ads, merely listing the availability of accounting services. Ads, such as these, gain little reader recognition, so the results are bound to be disappointing. Yet, from a media perspective, newspapers do possess several advantages.

The principal advantage of newspapers is their geographic, rather than demographic, selectivity. Metropolitan newspapers, and even such nationally circulated papers as The Wall Street Journal, offer city and zoned editions. These zoned editions are much cheaper to advertise in than the full-run edition. Also, many city newspapers have a separate business section, and of course there is a growing number of weekly business papers in the larger metropolitan markets. However, even business-oriented newspapers appeal to a demographically diverse market. This is not a problem, if your target markets are diverse, or if a considerable number of people within your targeted segments subscribe to the particular paper in question. For example, advertising tax preparation services in newspapers makes more sense than advertising lease/buy studies. There are far more people who have a need for a tax preparation service than those that have a need for the latter.

Two noteworthy disadvantages of newspapers are their short life span (they are read and quickly discarded) and the fact that your ad is competing for attention against hundreds of other ads.

Local newspapers make the most sense for a firm appealing to a diverse mix of clients who require less specialized services, such as periodic financial statement and payroll tax preparation. There is a market for these services, and of course some of these lead to the cross-selling of additional services. Also, those firms who wish to keep their paraprofessional staff fully employed should test the effectiveness of newspaper ads in promoting write-up work. Newspapers give the advertiser the potential for reaching a wide cross-section of people with both a high degree of frequency as well as continuity. However, a series of attractive ads in the smaller suburban and city papers can help a firm in gaining firm visibility and name recognition, whereas very little can be expected from any one ad, regardless of the circulation of the paper.

SELECTING AN ADVERTISING AGENCY

Specifically, what can an advertising agency do for you? An agency can furnish advice concerning the execution of the advertising strategy, compare alternative media, cost out the ads, recommend a budget allocation in keeping with the campaign objectives, and of course, design the advertisements. The responsibility of the agency is first to determine its client's promotional needs, ask qualifying questions, and learn about the nature of the business. Beware of agencies, consultants, or public relations firms that start the engagement with specific strategies already outlined. Remember that advertising agencies work best when clients come to them with a clear idea of what they wish to accomplish, and how they wish to measure it. The responsibility of a public accounting firm is to formulate a message theme and develop a profile of the intended market segments. Advertising agencies are not knowledgeable about the nature of your business or your clients' needs and motivations. Consequently, CPAs have the responsibility of determining the target market and the image they wish to project. The agency can then more intelligently select appropriate media and develop the requisite imagery.

Do you need an advertising agency? This depends on your specific situation. If you are going to develop a series of modest black and white newspaper ads promoting a specific service, then the newspaper will set the copy for you and design the ad. However, the paper is not going to spend a lot of time in developing graphic illustrations. The illustrations they use generally come from clip art files. Depending on the nature of your message, this could or could not be appropriate. If you plan to advertise in nationally or regionally distributed magazines, journals, or business newspapers, then these media generally require "camera ready" work. Also, this kind of advertising often relies on a higher degree of imagery than newspaper advertisements. If you plan to develop a rather elaborate direct mail campaign, then I recommend hiring a direct-response advertising agency that specializes in the intricacies of this form of advertising. More local, direct mail campaigns in which you are mailing an existing firm brochure, cover letter, and response card to a smaller group of people can often be done "in-house."

When hiring an agency, it would be helpful to commission an

agency that has experience in advertising public accounting services, or other professional service firms. However, this is not always possible. In fact, in most smaller communities the main business of agencies is to prepare promotional material (posters, brochures, and flyers). Unlike larger metropolitan advertising agencies, these smaller agencies do not deal as frequently with the design and development of imagery advertisements.

In conclusion, advertising does have a place in firms' practice development programs, but it is no panacea for promotional problems. There is an ordered process to follow when determining what to advertise and to whom. Additionally, decisions concerning which media to use and how frequently to advertise often involve many factors. In many instances the assistance of an advertising agency is necessary in making these decisions. A lot can go wrong in an advertising campaign, but if properly executed, advertising has the potential of reaching thousands of prospects with a uniform message. This potential relies primarily on the clear communication of a relevant message to a predetermined market, the selection of appropriate media, and the frequency and continuity of message placement. Any or all of these elements will work for or against you in the successful execution of an advertising campaign.

NOTES

1. Ellen Terry Kesster, "Advertising Accounting Services: How Effective Has It Been?" *The Practical Accountant*, July 1981, p. 40; *The Wall Street Journal*, April 15, 1980, p. 1.

2. Philip C. Neubauer, *CPA Marketing Report*, Atlanta, Ga., December 1982, p. 11; Martha Middleton, "Ad Campaign Fails, Law Firm Goes Bankrupt," *ABA Journal*, 1981, p. 25.

3. William R. George and Leonard L. Berry, "Guidelines for the Advertising of Services," *Business Horizons*, July/August 1981, pp. 52–56.

4. Irwin Braun, "Seven Major Mistakes Accountants Make in Advertising," *The CPA Journal*, July 1982, pp. 82–83.

5. Michael R. Skigen, "Advertising on a Limited Budget: A Small Firm's Experience," *The Practical Accountant*, October 1981, pp. 57–61.

The Role and Promise of Personal Selling in Marketing a Public Accounting Firm

"Client relationships begin with the sale."

In a very real sense our successes and failures in life often rely on our ability to influence the actions of others. **Selling**, simply stated, is the ability to favorably influence people. Clergy sell the tenets of their religion. Educators sell ideas. Politicians sell their programs and personal worth. CPAs sell their approaches to financial problems. Indeed, how we influence people in our daily lives relates closely to our personal welfare. It therefore behooves CPAs to develop those communication skills that allow them to favorably influence the actions of others. These communication skills are sought by management and demanded by a competitive marketplace.

As Table 9–1 indicates, personal selling is far more powerful in influencing the actions of others than mass communication. This is not to say that mass communication approaches are unimportant,

TABLE 9-1

**Personal Selling versus Mass Communication in Terms of
Persuasive Ability**

	Personal Selling	Mass Communication (Advertising, Publicity)
General characteristics of personal selling and advertising as promotional methods	1. Personal, face to face	1. Impersonal
	2. Flexible	2. Inflexible
	3. Individual approach	3. General approach
	4. Slow market penetration	4. Quick market penetration
	5. Costly presentation, usually to target customers	5. Economical presentation
	6. Two-way communication	6. One-way communication
	7. Possibility of rebuilding interest	7. One shot at developing interest
	8. Ideas tailored to customer	8. Limited number of general ideas
	9. Customer carried through reasoning process	9. Suggestions offered
	10. No limit on stimuli	10. Limited number of stimuli
	11. Much more control over	11. Little control over purchasing decision

for they also play a key part in practice development programs. However, developing effective personal selling skills is of critical importance for public accountants because they depend on these skills to sell their ideas. Unlike the popular myth, the world will not beat a path to the door of the firm offering the best product or service. Service quality alone has never been an assurance of market success, but it has always been one of its prerequisites.

What do clients consider in assessing service quality? Clients, in part, base their initial (as well as repurchase) decisions on their faith in you and how receptive you appear to be to the solution of their problems. Later, the quality of service rendered influences these clients' repurchase decisions. Their perception of service quality is strongly influenced by their interpersonal relationships with delivery personnel. For individual clients, rather than the market at large, decide which firms offer the best service and why. That is why developing effective sales skills is a must for each staff member. I have worked for and with professional service firms who have hired sales people to specifically prospect for new clients and develop sales presentations. I have never been totally comfortable with this arrangement either operationally or philosophically, for the greatest potential for growth rests in training staff how to sell the services they will later perform.[1] This is far better than trying to centralize sales responsibility.

In summary, clients' perceptions of the worth of the service are strongly influenced by the interpersonal skills of service suppliers. Sales skills are necessary to promote your services, as well as deliver the service. They are crucial in our day-to-day dealings with clients, for they help us explain, dramatize, articulate, and, yes, promote what we are all about.

THE ROLE OF AN ACCOUNTANT AS A SALESPERSON

The role of an accountant is one of a problem solver. Public accountants are external consultants who specialize in the identification of occasionally hidden financial problems. They also assume the role of an advisor who recommends viable solutions to these problems. Therefore, CPAs have to learn to qualify clients' needs, determine purchasing motives, assess service expectations, establish priorities, and inform nontechnical clients about what can be done. This is not solely an internalized thought process. However, problems occur when public accountants treat it as such and erroneously give the impression of being aloof to clients' concerns. Remember, when selling intangible services, there has to be an interactive, advisory relationship between staff and clients. Many clients have been lost because they felt they did not receive this kind of service, even though the technical quality of the service was high. For CPAs, commercial successes rely on their abilities to identify and articulate concerns that are important to their clients. This is precisely what most sales people do on a daily basis.

Many public accountants have a negative, stereotypical impression of salespeople, which some unfortunately equate with the efficacy of personal selling. Developing personal selling skills does not mean that public accountants have to act in an overly aggressive, mercantile manner. There is a difference between being an assertive, other-directed person, interested in solving clients' problems, versus the typical stereotype of the hard-sell salespeople. Most of us avoid overly aggressive salespeople and foster relationships with those who seem interested in helping us. In fact, research has shown that the most effective salespeople are the less flashy, analytical problem solvers versus the hard sell salespeople.[2]

In summary, clients are not just purchasing a technical write-up or report. This is just the tangible evidence of the service. What is being sold, as well as purchased, is the solutions to problems. Clients purchase solutions to their financial problems, which carry the expectations of benefits. Solutions, insights, alternatives— these are what you are actually selling. The performance of the technical service just happens to be your production process. In fact, the technical service is a staid commodity, so don't get overly concerned with selling production processes. Rather sell clients on the benefits accruing to them when their problems are identified and solved. This is an interactive process that strongly relies on the development of interpersonal communication skills.

Unique Problem of Selling Technical Services

As we discussed in Chapter 1, one of the most difficult things to sell is an intangible service. The more technical the service, the more difficult it is for nontechnical clients to identify important service benefits. Public accountants know what the benefits of particular service offerings are, but often first-time adopters of a service do not. Potential clients also have the added difficulty of trying to determine which firm is the best one to hire. In their minds the quality of the service relies on the execution of the service. When purchasing goods, consumers don't have this problem. Product quality is more readily observable and uniform among competitive vendors selling the same brand. Not so with a service. Accounting services are intangibles, with limited but specific appeal. They are also often shrouded by technical features difficult to explain to the uninitiated. This means that accountants must learn to explain their services in benefit-oriented terms rather than merely explain technicalities associated with the production process. Ideas, approaches, and recommendations need to be carefully discussed with clients before, after, and during the production of the service.

Traits of Effective Salespeople

The stereotypical salesperson is often thought of as a fast-talking, smiling, extrovert, with a gift of gab and an aggressive manner. We can see this in popularized images such as Professor Harold Hill in *The Music Man* and Willy Loman in *Death of a Salesman*. Ask people to describe a salesperson, and what kind of description will you get? Usually one of an extremely aggressive person, a fast talker, overly friendly, somewhat insincere, manipulative, and a person who pressures buyers into decisions. Yet, most companies selling to business people shy away from hiring people like this. Therefore, the point to conclude is that we should not equate salesmanship with a stereotype that isn't worth emulating. Rather, let's consider which traits more effective salespeople possess. Research has shown that the profile of highly successful salespeople cluster around these attributes: [3]

1. Effective communication skills, both verbal and listening skills.
2. Above average intelligence.
3. Drive and a high degree of self-confidence.
4. Empathy and a sense of other-directedness.
5. A high degree of "product" or technical knowledge.
6. Analytical problem solving skills.
7. Sales presentation skills, knowing when and how to close a sale, handle problem objections, and other like concerns.

Some of these are learned skills while others are more closely related to intrinsic personality features. Therefore, it is wrong to conclude that effective salespeople are born. Rather, like entrepreneurs, they possess some behavioral tendencies that they develop. Many accountants already possess some of these same attributes (such as items 2, 3, 4, 5, and 6) that characterize more successful salespeople. CPAs would not be able to survive in the highly demanding profession of public accounting, if they did not possess these skills. Skills 1 and 2 are learned skills, which can be developed. This does not mean that every accountant will be a "crackerjack" salesperson. Clearly, this is not the case, but sales skills can be taught, practiced, and refined. Consider the traits of the more successful salespeople within your own firms. No doubt they possess many of the same qualities we have been discussing, yet I doubt if they fit the stereotype of the hard-sell salesperson.

Some staff members will always be much better than others when it comes to interpersonal communication, and there will always be that group whose skills and contributions lie elsewhere. But most can improve their skills, if they have both the interest in doing so, and they know what to do. Later in this chapter we discuss specific guidelines and recommendations concerning how to develop more effective presentations. This will definitely help, but management must also build the expectations in the minds of

FIGURE 9-1

The Sales Loop

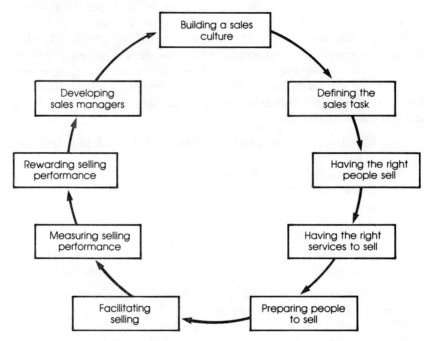

Source: Leonard L. Berry, Charles M. Futrell, and Michael R. Bowers, *Bankers Who Sell* (Homewood, Ill.: Dow Jones-Irwin, 1985), p. 144.

their employees that these are important skills to develop. This may mean that training programs will have to be developed in an attempt to develop these burgeoning skills.

Figure 9-1 describes the steps in the process of building an effective sales program. As indicated, building an operational sales culture first relies on stipulating the desired behavior. Management must then assign particular but varying tasks to different staff members. For example, the duties of partners and senior staff will be different from those of staff auditors and junior staff members in general. However, all will have some sales responsibilities. Also, in order to develop the desired sales culture into an organizational value, management must train employees before attempting to evaluate and reward performance.

DEVELOPING BASIC SALES SKILLS

The personal selling process depends on a number of basic skills public accountants can be trained to perform effectively. These skills pertain to the process of making personalized sales presentations to existing clients as well as prospects.

Not all encounters will really be opportunities to sell, but they will all be opportunities to interact. The skills needed to sell services are the same skills needed to effectively interact with clients. Let's now discuss some of these basic sales skills that staff can be taught to practice.

Precall Planning and Setting Call Objectives

Staff should have a clear communication goal in mind before they schedule a meeting with a client and identify the expected outcomes of that meeting. The probability of achieving an outcome relies strongly on initially identifying precisely what has to be accomplished. Effective planning necessitates first determining clients' needs, motives, interests, and objections to a particular course of action. Sometimes this can be accomplished before the meeting (**precall planning**). Often this behavioral information can only be determined during a meeting. With practice, this planning process becomes a learned pattern of behavior that positively affects service quality.

What are some specific examples of the types of considerations staff has to address? While not an exhaustive listing, the following are indicative of the types of considerations to address prior to or during client meetings.

1. Identify clients' problems and relate these problems to specific service offerings you need to discuss. Regularly assess clients' needs and concerns and communicate this to other staff members who also service that account.

2. Anticipate likely objections or questions clients may raise concerning your recommendations and prepare appropriate responses. Learn to anticipate likely objections by looking at problems from clients' perspectives.

3. Before a meeting, consider how you will dramatize and explain the service offerings in benefit-oriented terms. Work up a few examples or illustrations that support your recommendations.

4. Plan to build into the presentation client involvement via a

questioning approach and evaluative inquiries. Remember, it is difficult to determine how another perceives your point of view if that person offers little feedback.

5. Determine realistic call objectives to accomplish before a meeting. Then outline how to organize the presentation so as to accomplish these objectives. Some examples of call objectives, which will vary by one's familiarity with clients' needs, are the following:

- Qualifying service needs by obtaining some needed bit of information.
- Assessing interest in a particular service offering.
- Obtaining client commitment to a particular course of action.
- Arranging for another meeting with the key decision maker (KDM).
- Establishing a timetable for the completion of a particular task.

Establishing call objectives and then organizing a presentation in order to achieve them will often lead to an increase in billings as well as strengthened relationships with clients.

Qualifying Clients' Needs

Effective qualification, as Figure 9–2 indicates, involves three spheres of influence. This qualification process should occur throughout the engagement as you learn more about clients' needs and financial limitations. However, the majority of qualification inquiries should occur during the early stages of the initial meeting. Some clients will initially qualify themselves by identifying their service needs. Others will be far more reserved and guarded in their comments until a feeling of trust has been earned. In either extreme, the responsibility for qualification according to the three spheres of influence is the responsibility of the seller. Therefore, public accountants have to learn that qualification is both a continuous process and the principal call objective of the first meeting. They need to ask pointed questions and get clients involved in articulating their problems and concerns.

Developing Effective Listening Skills

Effective communication is an interactive process between two or more people. Developing refined listening skills is a very important part of this process. Frequently the business situation is such

FIGURE 9-2

Qualifying Prospects

Effective qualification involves three separate spheres of *inquiry:*

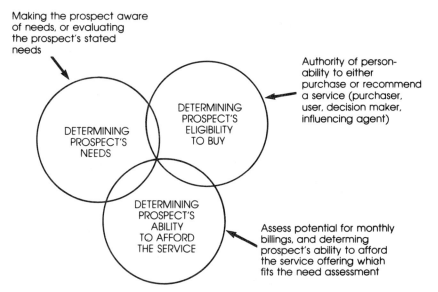

Making the prospect aware of needs, or evaluating the prospect's stated needs

DETERMINING PROSPECT'S NEEDS

DETERMINING PROSPECT'S ELIGIBILITY TO BUY

Authority of person-ability to either purchase or recommend a service (purchaser, user, decision maker, influencing agent)

DETERMINING PROSPECT'S ABILITY TO AFFORD THE SERVICE

Assess potential for monthly billings, and determing prospect's ability to afford the service offering which fits the need assessment

This qualification process is a CONTINUOUS process that should occur throughout the major body of the presentation. However, the majority of qualification inquiries should occur during the early stages of a presentation.

that a client couches his or her true feelings in socially accepted phrases or vagaries that can be taken literally. Consequently, delivery staff miss buying signals, hidden needs, purchasing motives, and fail to assess aptly a client's interests. These miscommunication problems can never be fully solved, but their impact and frequency of occurrence can be minimized. The following are some suggestions concerning how to minimize their impact.

1. Try not to dominate the conversation unless absolutely necessary, but rather learn to orchestrate its flow. Encourage the client's interaction by asking pertinent evaluative questions.

2. Watch the client's "body language" for the unstated or understated response.

3. Pause and categorize client's responses before reacting in a hasty manner. For example, some responses represent genuine

objections to recommendations, while others are merely "put off" objections. Whichever is the case, your response to an unexpected objection should be based on how you categorize that objection.

4. During your presentations learn to mentally summarize client's views and positions. This will help you become more empathetic with his or her position and anticipate unvocalized objections.

5. Train yourself not to become so caught up in the dialogue that you lose the objectivity necessary to control the conversation, rather than being controlled by it.

Creating Interactive Presentations

Effective communication means more than just being informative and persuasive. Success as a communicator necessitates developing both questioning and listening skills. Questions are excellent in providing feedback concerning what clients heard versus what was said. They can also be effectively used as trial closing techniques, evaluative inquiries, and methods for qualifying clients. Build in questions such as the following throughout your dialogue:

1. What is the possibility of starting this project in...?
2. Do I take it that you are in favor of this approach and would like me to initiate the process?
3. How would you characterize your present situation?
4. What is your principal reservation with...?

This questioning approach has three major benefits: (1) Provides you with prospect feedback concerning what has been communicated. (2) Gets clients involved in the discussion of their problems, rather than passive receivers of information. (3) Helps communicators determine what to say or emphasize next, which of course helps them to maintain control over presentations.

Translating Technical Features Into Benefits

Some clients, such as other accountants, may be interested in technical explanations of a service (e.g., audit procedures). For these clients the explanations represent a measure of service quality. However, most clients will not be interested in the technicalities. They assume CPAs possess the knowledge needed to perform the service and do not wish to be bothered with that which is uninteresting to them. This latter group is a more difficult group to sell than the former, for you have to translate technical service features into client benefits in order to establish the value of the service. There are no hard and fast ways of accomplishing this, but there are some guidelines to follow:

1. Begin the presentation by assessing the prospect's familiarity with the service offering. This will help indicate how technical your explanations need to be. But remember, even technically proficient clients will be interested in the identification of service benefits and expected outcomes.

2. Determine the client's dominant buying motive early in the qualification process. Whenever possible, relate technical service features with the dominant buying motive. This helps maintain client's interest throughout the presentation.

3. Persuade the client of the worth of your ideas with examples that do not violate the confidentiality of other clients. Similar case situations do give clients specific examples they can relate to, while also providing both substance and proof to your assertions.

4. Be sure to involve your client throughout the presentation. Help the client understand the benefits and features you have been discussing. Ask questions, invite inquiries, frequently summarize, and assess client's agreement with what has been discussed throughout the presentation. Remember, if there is little client involvement in the main body of your presentation, what kind of involvement can you expect when it is time to make a decision?

Using Visual Aids to Explain Your Ideas

There is far too great a reliance on the spoken word when selling technical services. Yet, psychological research tells us that people are generally able to recall only a small percentage of what they hear and less than 50 percent of what they read, but the majority of what they hear, see, and apply. Visual aids, therefore, have the potential to help convey meaning and can greatly influence the perception of a message. Visual aids focus clients' attention on specific items or concerns that need to be emphasized or explained, and they help to structure the presentation. They also help clients in applying somewhat abstract ideas because they are able to visually conceptualize what another is explaining. Additionally, visual aids can be quite helpful in group presentations where the dialogue is not on a one-to-one basis. Remember, clients' decisions are going to be based on what they perceived and remembered, so it is important to convey your message in as readily an understandable manner as possible. Table 9–2 contains a listing of some frequently overlooked visual aids that are flexible enough to use in a variety of situations.

TABLE 9–2

Suggested Uses of Visual Aids

1. Paper and pencil illustrations or listings.   For example, as you discuss the attributes of a service or alternative courses of action, jot down the pros/cons in a T-account format. This helps focus the client's attention concerning what to consider when making a decision.

2. Pamphlets and firm brochures.   Circle, check, or highlight key points within the text either during your presentation or beforehand. Discuss these considerations with the client and leave this high-lighted material for his or her review.

3. Prepared flowcharts and illustrations.   For example, prepare a laminated flowchart of the steps your audit teams go through when conducting certain types of audits. This chart can then be incorporated into a sales presentation. A printed copy of this aid can be left with the client as a reference piece.

4. Transparency overlays.   These can be quite helpful when making personalized group presentations, such as in the management services area where you need to discuss the findings of a study. Transparencies can be made of key pages of the report, which aids both in the structuring of the presentation and the discussion of pertinent conclusions and recommendations.

5. Sales presentation book.   Some firms find it helpful to have laminated pages concerning fee schedules, firm policy statements, areas of specific expertise, grouped services, and flowchart illustrations all bound together and indexed in a presentation book. Then, when incorporating this material in a presentation, staff can write directly on these pages with an erasable transparency marker.

Handling Clients' Objections

The basic rule to follow is to welcome client objections as a sign of interest. Categorize them before you answer, address the objection, and then return to the discussion. Why are client objections so important? Well, have you ever tried to convince someone of your point of view who refused to actively engage in a conversation? The parallel extends to selling because the toughest clients to close are the ones who raise no objections. With most service engagements there are bound to be aspects of the engagement prospective clients express a concern over. Clients' objections are therefore important because they allow CPAs to accomplish the following:

1. Assess client's interest in what has been explained.
2. Obtain feedback concerning a client's understanding of what has been communicated.
3. Further qualify client's needs and interests.
4. Actively involve client in the discussion of his or her problems.

Clients' objections are therefore a normal part of the communication process, and public accountants have to learn to expect them. Unfortunately, many CPAs classify objections in one or more of the following ways:

1. Affronts against their credibility and self-worth.
2. Obstacles to avoid, not address, in a sales presentation.
3. Severe impediments to closing a sale or obtaining client agreement.
4. Unwanted social confrontations that are awkward.

Consequently, they don't consider clients' objections as a sign of interest or as an opportunity to further explain their point of view. The importance of objections can be further clarified by conceptualizing what has caused the client to raise the objection in the first place. Objections can be caused by something the CPA has either said or omitted. For example, a failure to qualify the clients needs, establish rapport early in the presentation, or relate service features to benefits are all omissions that may well cause clients to raise objections. Fortunately these objections provide service suppliers with the needed degree of feedback to remedy these situations.

Objections can be based on either rational or emotional motives. Both are equally important and, consequently, need to be addressed. For example, clients' natural tendencies to resist spending are based on a rational motive, whereas a reluctance to make a decision, personal antagonism, or an aversion to change are all based on emotional motives. Both have to be identified, understood for what they are, and addressed before a favorable decision can be made.

Table 9–3 describes one method of classifying objections before answering them, and Table 9–4 lists some techniques for countering clients' objections. Again, these are skills most staff members can be taught in training programs. These training programs can be taught by partners and managers who are highly successful in presenting proposals and dealing with clients on a one-to-óne basis. Outside instructors can also be used to develop these important skills, if expertise is lacking within your own organization.

TABLE 9–3

Classifying Objections

Before answering an objection and responding to what you think the buyer is saying, first categorize the objection. This process will help you determine a more effective reply than a spontaneous reaction to the objection.

1. **Stated objections** are overt points of resistance to overcome when they are raised. Most of the time they are valid objections, but occasionally they mask the real objection (objecting to price, when the real objection concerns the prospect's perceived need for the service). You have to *think* about the objection and evaluate the buyer's response before answering the objection.

   Real objection: "Why should I hire your firm that has a reputation of having considerably higher fees rather than another competent public accounting firm?"

   Artificial objection: "I am not ready to act now, so why don't we call it a day, and I will contact you later."

   You have to find out what the real objection is and verbalize it before you can effectively counteract it and move toward closing.

2. **Unstated objections** are those points of resistance the buyer has not vocalized, but are nevertheless severe obstacles to closing the sale. They have to be stated before you can counteract them so the burden falls upon you, not the buyer, in bringing them to the forefront. Watch the "body language," be aware of periods of silence and changes in behavior. These are your indicators of unstated objections. Probe for these through direct questioning so you can turn the unstated into a stated objection.

   "Mr. Jones, how would you evaluate this service offering in terms of fitting your needs?"

   "Are you concerned about the confidentiality of our relationship?"

3. **Hopeless objections** are those objections which cannot be answered or should not be answered.

   Cannot answer:

   "I am not interested in your service because I recently signed a contract with a competitor of yours whom I am quite pleased with."

   Should not answer:

   Some objections should be avoided because the buyer in haste states something he or she does not believe. Sometimes it is best not to make an issue of that faux pas. These situations are rare, and your intuition will tell you when they occur.

TABLE 9–4

Methods for Answering Objections

1. Agree and qualify (explain).
2. Turn the objection into a selling point (reverse).
3. Agree that the objection is valid (admit).
4. Delay answering the objection (delay).
5. Ignore the objection (highly selective use).
6. Politely deny that the objection is valid (deny).
7. Ask questions for further explanation (qualify).

Learning How to Get Clients to Say Yes

Sales people call this process of obtaining agreement **closing**. Closing is a continuous process, not an event, although many CPAs think of closing as what happens at the end of the presentation. It is precisely this view that causes them to fear the closing process, for it places the risk on that last act of asking for the engagement. Consequently, public accountants often fear or dread closing for these principal reasons:

1. Fear of clients saying no.
2. Viewing "no" decisions as personal rejections of themselves.
3. Feeling uncertain about how to close.
4. A belief that assertively asking for engagements will make social relationships between clients and CPAs awkward.

Closing is a continuous process. If done effectively, you will be testing clients' receptivities to what you are recommending throughout the presentations by using trial closing techniques. A **trial close** is a type of "trial balloon" that provides you with feedback concerning clients' interests with what has been stated. When using trial closing techniques, you are building a series of subtle acceptances, ascertaining degrees of agreement, probing for hidden objections, and determining if clients are ready to close. Sellers of all technical services have to determine if clients are ready to close, because most clients will not close themselves. This can be accomplished through the use of subtle trial closes leading to the final closing act of asking for the engagement. This is done only after you have successfully assessed a client's readiness to act through the use of trial closes.

Trial closes can be used at almost any time throughout the presentation, but some of the more appropriate times to execute a trial close are these:

1. After dramatizing a strong selling point of the service.
2. After obtaining agreement on a key aspect of the service.
3. After successfully answering an important objection.
4. When the client gives you an important closing signal.
5. Before moving on to the next phase of a presentation.
6. When you need client feedback concerning what has been presented.

Most clients will indicate throughout the presentation their receptivities towards what has been stated. Don't worry about losing "the opportunity" to trial close as there will often be many opportunities. Rather, make sure that trial closes do not appear too awkward or direct. Overtly asking for the engagement too early in the presentation can be perceived by clients as too aggressive. Rather, it is better to build a series of acceptances or agreements into the presentation before asking for the engagement. Table 9–5 lists some sample trial closing techniques to experiment with. Some other more subtle techniques to consider follow that presentation.

THE SALES PRESENTATION PROCESS

Developing effective sales presentations strongly depends on first obtaining client attention and interest early in the presentation. Creating interest is necessary before you can reasonably expect clients to develop desire for services. After the desire stage, clients are more likely to make a purchase decision. Salespeople have developed an acronym called AIDA, which stands for this ordered process of first obtaining prospect *attention*, then creating *interest* in what you are selling, before stimulating *desire* and *action* (see Table 9–6). Of key importance in this developmental process is to help your clients determine how the service offering solves their problems. In order to do this, you have to assess their motives, determine their needs, and recommend benefit-oriented solutions to their problems.

Presentations do substantially differ from situation to situation and depend on the encountered circumstances. There is no such thing as a model process to follow in every encounter. What will be accomplished, whether you ought to even recommend a specific service to a client or prospect, as well as the speed in which you progress, will vary by situation. In some instances, the client will

TABLE 9-5

Trial Closing Techniques

The technique has to fit the situation. There is no such thing as the best closing technique. Nevertheless, here are several proven techniques that you will find make trial closing and the actual closing statement a lot easier.

1. Assume the sale is made _____

2. Build a series of acceptances _____

3. Summarize the key selling points _____

4. Obtain decisions on pertinent points _____

5. Use the what if. . .or contingent method _____

6. The impending event or critical incident method _____

7. The alternative decision or counterpoint method _____

8. The direct approach by overtly asking for the engagement _____

9. The T-account approach followed by asking for the engagement _____

Consider the client's needs and reactions. Let that person set the pace, but you control the interview and pick up on the "closing signals." If the trial close meets with resistance, it does not mean the sale is lost. It merely indicates at that point the prospective client is not ready to make an affirmative decision. There is some objection that needs to be answered before another decision is attempted, so you better determine it before trying another closing technique.

approach your firm and make his or her interest and needs known. An agreement to complete the service by a specified date may be the logical outcome of this first meeting. In other situations, it may take several visits just to assess the prospect's needs and meet with the necessary influence agents and decision makers. Therefore, there is no such thing as a mechanistic process that has to be followed in every situation. Yet, there is a logical progression of activities that can, in many instances, be prudent to follow. Let's consider this ordered process, which could be changed by specific

TABLE 9-6

Four Criteria for Effective Sales Presentations

1. YOUR PRESENTATION MUST CAPTURE THE PROSPECT'S ATTENTION.

    Consider a strong attention-getting lead-in and plan to use this in the beginning of the presentation. Conceptualize this lead-in by determining key buying motives.

2. THE PRESENTATION MUST AROUSE INTEREST.

    Does the service that you are presenting offer the buyer basic benefits? If so, overtly discuss these benefits. Don't just discuss staid features, rather, relate features to benefits.

3. THE PRESENTATION MUST STIMULATE DESIRE FOR YOUR SERVICE.

    Discuss problems to be solved (present and future) and relate how the solving of these problems provides basic benefits of interest to the buyer.

4. FINALLY, THE PRESENTATION MUST MOTIVATE THE BUYER TO TAKE ACTION

    Obtain frequent buyer agreement on small points and involve the buyer in the presentation through pointed questioning. Also, direct the buyer to summarize and evaluate a situation so as to help you ascertain buyer acceptance of your ideas.

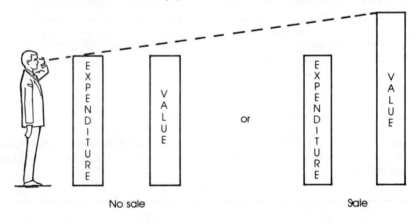

situations, but which, nevertheless, does outline a logical approach to follow.

Stage One: Preparation Stage

In this stage, give initial consideration to prospecting for clients who have the need for and financial abilities to afford specific services. Frequently, this form of prospecting involves a formal process of generating leads and then screening prospective clients against some established criteria. Another form of prospecting involves an internal review of the needs of existing clients and a determination of which clients ought to be targeted for select service offerings. In either case, identify targeted clients and assess their service needs and perceived receptivities toward the service. Before meeting with these prospects, determine specific sales call objectives and briefly outline the considerations that need to be addressed in the forthcoming presentations. Identify points of sale resistance and likely objections in this preparation stage, as well as ways of addressing these concerns.

Stage Two: Presentation Stage

First, qualify the prospect on the three spheres of influence we discussed earlier in this chapter. This qualification process is necessary before proceeding further in the presentation, although clients' real needs and limitations often become identifiable only as the presentation progresses. Therefore, qualification, like trial closing, is a continuous process rather than an event. After qualification, then discuss specific service recommendations. Sometimes these are the same services you planned to sell. Other times, your initial assessments prove not to be in the best interest of the client. In such cases, it is necessary to immediately modify and reconceptualize what you need to accomplish. In either instance, follow qualification by an identification and discussion of service needs.

The majority of prospects will raise objections during the early to mid part of the presentation. This is also the time to execute trial closes. The objective of this stage is to move qualified prospects toward an evaluative decision, which hopefully will be in the affirmative.

Stage Three: Transaction Stage

This is the point in the presentation process that you ask the prospect for the engagement. This should be a natural and logical progression from the presentation stage. If it is not, do not proceed further because the prospect is not ready to make a decision. Generally, what needs to be done is to uncover unstated objections, deal with the clients' concerns, requalify their needs and interests, and review service benefits. What you are trying to avoid is to force a client into a premature decision. Remember, when people are not ready to act, it is far easier for them to say no than it is to respond in the affirmative. Usually a "yes" decision carries more risk for unpersuaded clients than a negative response. This last stage, like the others, can take more than one meeting.

NOTES

1. Warren J. Wittreich, "How to Buy/Sell Professional Services," *Harvard Business Review*, March–April 1966, p. 129.

2. Robert R. Blake and Jane Srygley Mouton, *The Grid for Sales Excellence: Benchmarks for Effective Salesmanship* (New York: McGraw-Hill, 1970).

3. For a more detailed review of the characteristics of successful sales personnel see Bradley D. Lockeman and John H. Hallaq, "Who Are Your Successful Salespeople?" *Journal of Academy of Marketing Science* 10 (Fall 1982), pp. 457–471.

INDEX